THE CASE FOR
Christ

—

STUDY GUIDE
Revised Edition

Resources by Lee Strobel

The Case for Christ
The Case for Christ audio
The Case for Christ Student Edition (with Jane Vogel)
The Case for Christ curriculum (with Garry Poole)
The Case for Christmas
The Case for Christmas audio
The Case for a Creator
The Case for a Creator audio
The Case for Creator Student Edition (with Jane Vogel)
The Case for a Creator curriculum (with Garry Poole)
The Case for Easter
The Case for Faith
The Case for Faith audio
The Case for Faith Student Edition (with Jane Vogel)
The Case for Faith curriculum (with Garry Poole)
The Case for the Real Jesus
The Case for the Real Jesus audio
Faith Under Fire curriculum
God's Outrageous Claims
Inside the Mind of Unchurched Harry and Mary
Off My Case for Kids
Surviving a Spiritual Mismatch in Marriage (with Leslie Strobel)
Surviving a Spiritual Mismatch in Marriage audio
What Jesus Would Say

Other Resources by Garry Poole

The Complete Book of Questions
Seeker Small Groups

In the Tough Questions Series:

Don't All Religions Lead to God?
How Could God Allow Suffering and Evil?
How Does Anyone Know God Exists?
Why Become a Christian?
Tough Questions Leader's Guide (with Judson Poling)

THE CASE FOR
Christ

—

*Investigating the Evidence
for Jesus*

LEE
STROBEL

NEW YORK TIMES BESTSELLING AUTHOR

AND GARRY POOLE

Revised Edition

ZONDERVAN

The Case for Christ Study Guide Revised Edition
Copyright © 2008, 2013 by Lee Strobel and Garry Poole

This title is also available as a Zondervan ebook.
Visit www.zondervan.com/ebooks.

Requests for information should be addressed to:

Zondervan, *Grand Rapids, Michigan 49530*

ISBN 978-0-310-69850-0

Cover design: Faceout Studio
Cover photography: Shutterstock®
Interior design: Beth Shagene

Printed in the United States of America

HB 05.21.2024

Contents

Special thanks to
Laura Allen and Jim Poole
for their outstanding writing and editorial contributions.
Their creative insights and suggestions
took this guide to the next level.

The Investigation
of a Lifetime

For much of my life I was a skeptic. In fact, I considered myself an atheist. To me, there was far too much evidence that God was merely a product of wishful thinking, of ancient mythology, of primitive superstition ... It wasn't a phone call from an informant that prompted me to reexamine the case for Christ. It was my wife ... Eventually I wanted to get to the bottom of what was prompting the subtle but significant shifts in my wife's attitudes, so I launched an all-out investigation into the facts surrounding the case for Christianity ... I applied the training I had received at Yale Law School as well as my experience as legal affairs editor of the Chicago Tribune. *And I plunged into the case with more vigor than with any story I had ever pursued.*

Lee Strobel, *The Case for Christ*

Read This!

If possible, read the introduction, Reopening the Investigation of a Life-time, in *The Case for Christ* book in preparation for this session. Otherwise, read it as follow-up.

Watch This!

Video Teaching Segment

Space is provided to take notes on anything that stands out to you.

Discuss This!

1. To what degree can you relate to the comments people made about Jesus in the video segment? What best represents your current position regarding what you believe about Jesus Christ?

"I don't believe we'll ever know if Jesus was really what everyone says he was. I think it's a lot of folklore. I think it's a lot of historical misrepresentation. It's a lot of wishful thinking. But I don't think we know. I don't think we'll ever know. And I don't think there's any way to prove what has been claimed about Jesus for all these years."
— Woman on the street

THINK ABOUT THIS!

"So, then, Christ may be said to be a fiction in the four senses that (1) it is quite possible that there was no historical Jesus; (2) even if there was, he is lost to us, the result being that there is no historical Jesus available to us; (3) the Jesus who "walks with me and talks with me and tells me I am his own" is an imaginative visualization and in the nature of the case can be nothing more than a fiction; and finally, (4) "Christ" as a corporate logo for this and that religious institution is a euphemistic fiction, not unlike Ronald McDonald, Mickey Mouse, or Joe Camel, the purpose of which is to get you to swallow a whole raft of beliefs, attitudes, and behaviors by an act of simple faith, short-circuiting the dangerous process of thinking the issues out to your own conclusions."

Marshall J. Gauvin, *Did Jesus Christ Really Live?*

"If Jesus Christ is only a human being — no matter how splendid a specimen of humanity he may be — he is part of the problem, not its solution."

British theologian Alister McGrath

"Historically, it is quite doubtful whether Christ ever existed at all, and if he did we do not know anything about him."

Atheist Bertrand Russell

2. What level of confidence do you have that Jesus is an actual historical figure? How confident are you that the existence of Jesus Christ is a matter of legend or wishful thinking? Give reasons behind your response.

"Jesus? I would say no doubt he lived as a person but to the extent of what he did, I'm not sure."
— Woman on the street

3. To what extent have you investigated the claims of Christianity prior to this discussion? Describe your experience.

"I have a lot of different thoughts and theories on Jesus, but I don't think coming back from the dead is really possible."
— Man on the street

4. While still an atheist, Lee's initial conclusion was this: *If Christianity is true, it has huge implications for one's life.* What do you think he meant by this statement? Do you agree or disagree with his assessment? Why?

"If Jesus is to be believed —
and I realize that may
be a big if for you at this
point — then nothing is
more important than how
you respond to him."
— Lee Strobel

THINK ABOUT THIS!

One Solitary Life

"He was born in an obscure village, the child of a peasant woman. He grew up in another obscure village, where he worked in a carpenter shop until he was thirty. Then for three years he was an itinerant preacher. He never had a family or owned a home. He never set foot inside a big city. He never traveled two hundred miles from the place he was born. He never wrote a book, or held an office. He did none of the things that usually accompany greatness.

"While he was still a young man, the tide of popular opinion turned against him. His friends deserted him. He was turned over to his enemies and went through the mockery of a trial. He was nailed to a cross between two thieves. While he was dying, his executioners gambled for the only piece of property he had — his coat.

"When he was dead, he was taken down and laid in a borrowed grave.

"Nineteen long centuries have come and gone, and today he is the central figure for much of the human race. All the armies that ever marched, and all the navies that ever sailed, and all the parliaments that ever sat, and all the kings that ever reigned, put together, have not affected the life of man upon this earth as powerfully as that one solitary life."

Author unknown

5. What do you believe about Jesus? Was he a great moral teacher? Was he a prophet? Did he possess special powers? Was he God in human form or was he simply a good man that legend has elevated to the status of the divine?

THINK ABOUT THIS!

"A man who was merely a man and said the sort of things Jesus said would not be a great moral teacher. He would either be a lunatic — on the level with the man who says he is a poached egg — or else he would be the Devil of Hell. You must make your choice. Either this was, and is, the Son of God; or else a madman or something worse. You can shut him up for a fool, you can spit at him and kill him as a demon, or you can fall at his feet and call him Lord and God. But let us not come with any patronizing nonsense about his being a great human teacher. He has not left that open to us. He did not intend to."

C. S. Lewis, *Mere Christianity*

6. Did Jesus really claim to be God? What did his followers of that era believe about his identity? What have you heard or read about the divinity of Jesus?

> *"Jesus made it clear by word and deed that to know him was to know God, to see him was to see God, to believe in him was to believe in God, to receive him was to receive God, to reject him was to reject God, and to honor him was to honor God."*
> — British theologian John Stott

7. Jesus once asked his disciples, "Who do the crowds say I am?" and he received a variety of responses (see Luke 9:18–19). At this point in your spiritual investigation, who do *you* say Jesus is? On a scale from 1 to 10 (1 = I'm very certain Jesus was an extraordinary man, but he was not God in human form; 5 = I'm in a fog concerning who Jesus was; 10 = I'm very certain Jesus was God in human form just as he claimed he was), place an X near the spot that best describes you. Then share your selection with the rest of the group and give reasons for placing your X where you did.

1	2	3	4	5	6	7	8	9	10

Jesus — a great man but not God   Unsure who Jesus was   Jesus — God in human form

OPTIONAL DISCUSSION QUESTIONS
for Those Investigating Christianity

- To what degree of accuracy do you think historical records can reflect actual past occurrences? What factors determine the level of accuracy of historical documents?

- Can we ever really know the historical truth about Jesus? Why or why not? What factors would increase the accuracy of our understanding of who Jesus is?

- In the video clip, Lee and Leslie Strobel shared aspects of their spiritual stories. Lee had antagonistic attitudes toward both Christians and Christianity, while Leslie was more neutral about the issues and uncertain about what she believed. Which of the two stories do you relate to most and why?

- Generally speaking, are you driven more by your head or by your heart? How might that impact your examination of the evidence for Christ? To what degree are your questions or objections about God a "heart issue" — as they were for Leslie — and to what degree is your spiritual journey a "head issue," which requires facts and documentation, like Lee?

- In what ways do Christians repel you from Christianity? In what ways, if any, do they attract you?

- Do you know anyone who has made the decision to become a Christian in the time that you've known them? If so, in what ways has he or she become a different person? How has their decision affected your relationship? What are some of the positive and negative changes that you observe?

- What is your assessment of the Bible? Is it a trustworthy historical document? Does it have any spiritual value? Give reasons for your answers.

- Regardless of whether or not you believe the Bible to be true, many have observed that it is a remarkable and beautiful piece of literature that has influenced countless generations. Aside from its potential spiritual value, is this reason enough to read and study it? Why or why not?

Between Sessions

Personal Reflection

> *It was now winter, and Jesus was in Jerusalem at the time of Hanukkah. He was at the Temple, walking through the section known as Solomon's Colonnade. The Jewish leaders surrounded him and asked, "How long are you going to keep us in suspense? If you are the Messiah, tell us plainly."*
>
> *Jesus replied, "I have already told you, and you don't believe me. The proof is what I do in the name of my Father. But you don't believe me because you are not part of my flock. My sheep recognize my voice; I know them, and they follow me. I give them eternal life, and they will never perish. No one will snatch them away from me, for my Father has given them to me, and he is more powerful than anyone else. So no one can take them from me. The Father and I are one."*
>
> *Once again the Jewish leaders picked up stones to kill him. Jesus said, "At my Father's direction I have done many things to help the people. For which one of these good deeds are you killing me?" They replied, "Not for any good work, but for blasphemy, because you, a mere man, have made yourself God."*
>
> John 10:22–33 NLT

1. Prior to this study session, when was the last time you gave more than a cursory thought to the person known as Jesus Christ? What impact has Jesus had in your life? And how did this humble man from the Middle East manage to revolutionize the entire known world in such a dramatic way that his very birthday divides all of history right down the middle?

2. What are some other ways Jesus has had influence — either positive or negative? How well have Christians followed the ways of Jesus?

3. Are the first four books of the New Testament — Matthew, Mark, Luke, and John — accurate biographies of the life and teachings of Jesus? How can you be sure?

4. According to John 10:22–33, what did Jesus appear to believe about himself? What do you think his followers believed about him? What did the religious leaders of that time believe about him?

5. British philosopher C. S. Lewis famously proposed that Jesus was either a legend, liar, lunatic, or the Lord God. Are there any other options? Would a sane, truthful, good person falsely claim to be God?

6. If you haven't already, how open are you to discovering the identity of Jesus for yourself once and for all? What is the driving force behind your search? What difference might it make in your life? And how committed are you to carefully examining the evidence and the facts of this case?

7. Perhaps you can take some time right now to further reflect on the verses written by the disciple John. Assuming this account has been preserved accurately, does it have anything new to teach you that you didn't already know about Jesus? Are you willing to say a short prayer right now to invite God to reveal the truth about Jesus to you in the coming days?

Personal Reading

Please read the following book content in preparation for session two:

The Case for Christ, chapter 1: The Eyewitness Evidence

The Case for Christ, chapter 2: Testing the Eyewitness Evidence

The Case for Christ, chapter 3: The Documentary Evidence

Eyewitness Evidence

But all I had ever really given the evidence was a cursory look. I had read just enough philosophy and history to find support for my skepticism — a fact here, a scientific theory there, a pithy quote, a clever argument ... Setting aside my self-interest and prejudices as best I could, I read books, interviewed experts, asked questions, analyzed history, explored archaeology, studied ancient literature, and for the first time in my life picked apart the Bible verse by verse.

Lee Strobel, *The Case for Christ*

Watch This!

Video Teaching Segment

Space is provided to take notes on anything that stands out to you.

Discuss This!

1. What's your assessment of the Bible? Is the Bible mostly accurate, partly accurate, or mostly inaccurate? Give reasons for your response.

"All Bibles are man-made."
— Thomas Edison

THINK ABOUT THIS!

"If we can have confidence that the Gospels were written by the disciples Matthew and John, by Mark, the companion of the disciple Peter, and by Luke, the historian, companion of Paul, and a first-century journalist, we can be assured that the events they record are based on either direct or indirect eyewitness testimony."

Lee Strobel

"Few intelligent Christians can still hold to the idea that the Bible is an infallible book, that it contains no linguistic errors, no historical discrepancies, no antiquated scientific assumptions, not even bad ethical standards. Historical investigation and literary criticism have taken the magic out of the Bible and have made it a composite human book, written by many hands in different ages. The existence of thousands of variations of texts makes it impossible to hold the doctrine of a book verbally infallible. Some might claim for the original copies of the Bible an infallible character, but this view only begs the question and makes such Christian apologetics more ridiculous in the eyes of the sincere man."

Elmer Homrighausen, former dean of Princeton Theological Seminary

2. Do you agree that the Bible is a set of ancient historical documents to which historians can apply the same criteria for determining whether or not *any* historical record is accurate? Elaborate.

"If God wanted to send us a message, and ancient writings were the only way he could think of doing it, he could have done a better job."
— Dr. Arroway in Carl Sagan's film *Contact*

"But what eyewitness accounts do we possess? Do we have the testimony of anyone who personally interacted with Jesus, who listened to his teachings, who saw his miracles, who witnessed his death, and who perhaps even encountered him after his alleged resurrection? Do we have any records from first-century 'journalists' who interviewed eyewitnesses, asked tough questions, and faithfully recorded what they scrupulously determined to be true? Equally important, how well would these accounts withstand the scrutiny of skeptics?"

Lee Strobel

"We have actually very early attestation of the authorship of the Gospels. The early church father Papias, for example, as recorded by the church historian Eusebius, identifies Mark's gospel as essentially the eyewitness account of Peter. Papias was a disciple of the apostle John, so we are only one generation removed from Jesus himself. Now that is a pretty close testimony and strongly suggesting that the Gospels are based on eyewitness accounts."

New Testament scholar Mark Strauss

"It has become evident to scholars of the first century that the Gospels were actually attempts to write biographies of Jesus. They are very clearly attempts by eyewitnesses to describe exactly what Jesus said and did, and the consensus of New Testament scholarship has moved in that direction."

Theologian and apologist J. P. Moreland

3. Read the introduction to the gospel of Luke, below:

> *Many have undertaken to draw up an account of the things that have been fulfilled among us, just as they were handed down to us by those who from the first were eyewitnesses and servants of the word. With this in mind, since I myself have carefully investigated everything from the beginning, I too decided to write an orderly account for you, most excellent Theophilus, so that you may know the certainty of the things you have been taught.*
>
> Luke 1:1–4

Would you agree or disagree that this appears to be the work of a biographer who has done his research? Elaborate.

THINK ABOUT THIS!

"Luke's gospel begins with a prologue; it is actually one of the finest Greek sections in the whole New Testament. Luke was clearly a literary artist, but in that prologue he points out that he has carefully investigated the material that he presents in the Gospels, that he has checked with eyewitness accounts, those who were actually present. If you read that prologue, you see that this is the work of a historian. This was someone who has done his research."

Mark Strauss

---

4. Mark Strauss suggests that the four New Testament Gospels or biographies of Jesus (Matthew, Mark, Luke, and John), all written in the first century, are our earliest and most reliable records of Jesus. Since they were written remarkably close to the actual occurrence of the events themselves, eyewitnesses still living and present would have objected to

any inaccuracies, making the Gospels unlikely to be corrupted by legend and wishful thinking. Do you agree or disagree with Strauss's logic? Why?

THINK ABOUT THIS!

"Consider the way the Gospels are written — in a sober and responsible fashion, with accurate incidental details, with obvious care and exactitude. You don't find the outlandish flourishes and blatant mythologizing that you see in a lot of other ancient writings."

New Testament scholar Craig Blomberg

---

5. How is your view of the level of accuracy behind the oral tradition influenced by the fact that in the tradition of the Jews — the culture in which Jesus lived — information was painstakingly and accurately preserved to the point that young rabbis were often forbidden to comment on a passage of Scripture until they had memorized it perfectly? In what ways does this approach differ from the game of "telephone" mentioned in the video clip? Elaborate.

"In no other case is the interval of time between the composition of the book and the date of the earliest manuscripts so short as in that of the New Testament."

— British classical scholar
Sir Frederic Kenyon

THINK ABOUT THIS!

"One of the arguments I'd often heard against believing what the Gospels say is that they contradict one another (see chart). How can two Gospels both be accurate if they give different accounts of the same event? A surprising discovery is that many historians consider minor variations to be evidence in favor of the truth of an account. The idea is that if the writers were lying, they'd make sure to get their stories straight — and they'd agree in every detail. What seems to be a contradiction is often just the same event viewed from a different perspective."

Lee Strobel

Story	Contradiction?	Possible Explanation
Jesus heals a Roman centurion's servant (described in Matthew 8:5 – 13 and Luke 7:1 – 10).	• Matthew says that the centurion asked Jesus to heal his servant. • Luke says that the centurion sent others to ask Jesus to heal the servant.	Just as we might say, "The president announced a new foreign policy today," when actually the announcement was written by a speechwriter and delivered by the press secretary, so in New Testament times people would say that an official (like the centurion) did something, even though he did it through others.
Jesus' genealogies (found in Matthew 1:1 – 16 and Luke 3:23 – 38).	Different people are listed in the two genealogies.	Matthew gives Joseph's side of the family tree; Luke gives Mary's side of the family tree.

If you're interested in studying other apparent contractions in the New Testament for yourself, consider either *The Encyclopedia of Biblical Difficulties* by Gleason L. Archer or *When Critics Ask* by Norman Geisler and Thomas Howe.

6. To what extent do you think the information contained in the original Bible manuscripts has been reliably copied and accurately translated into our current Bible? How much do you trust that the Bible you read today is an accurate reflection of the original intent?

"There is enough of a discrepancy to show that there could have been no previous concert among the [Gospel writers]; and at the same time such substantial agreement as to show that they all were independent narrators of the same great transaction."

— Simon Greenleaf, Harvard Law School

THINK ABOUT THIS!

"There is no comparison: the manuscript evidence for the New Testament is overwhelming when juxtaposed against other revered writings of antiquity — works that modern scholars have absolutely no reluctance treating as authentic. The grand total of Greek manuscripts is at 5,664. In addition to the Greek documents there are thousands of other ancient New Testament manuscripts in other languages. There are 8,000 to 10,000 Latin Vulgate manuscripts, plus a total of 8,000 in Ethiopic, Slavic, and Armenian. In all, there are about 24,000 manuscripts in existence."

Lee Strobel

Ancient Manuscripts
How the Numbers Stack up

9

The Jewish War by 1st-century historian, Josephus

30

Plato's writings

650

Homer's *Iliad*

24,000

New Testament

"The more often you have copies that agree with each other, especially if they emerge from different geographical areas, the more you can cross-check them to figure out what the original document was like. The only way they'd agree would be where they went back genealogically in a family tree that represents the descent of the manuscripts. The quantity of New Testament material is almost embarrassing in comparison with other works of antiquity."

Bruce Metzger, professor emeritus, Princeton Theological Seminary

7. How does the fact that there are virtually 24,000 copies of New Testament manuscripts affect your opinion about whether the texts we have are accurate?

THINK ABOUT THIS!

"Books — or actually, scrolls of papyrus — were relatively rare. Therefore education, learning, worship, teaching in religious communities — all this was done by word of mouth. Rabbis became famous for having the entire Old Testament committed to memory. So it would have been well within the capability of Jesus' disciples to have committed much more to memory than appears in all four Gospels put together — and to have passed it along accurately."

New Testament scholar Craig Blomberg

"The New Testament, then, has not only survived in more manuscripts than any other book from antiquity, but it has survived in a purer form than any other great book — a form that is 99.5 percent pure."

Norman Geisler and William Nix

"I've made a hobby of collecting alleged discrepancies, inaccuracies, and conflicting statements in the Bible. I have a list of about eight hundred of them. A few years ago I coauthored a book called When Critics Ask, which devotes nearly six hundred pages to setting the record straight. All I can tell you is that in my experience when critics raise these objections, they invariably violate one of seventeen principles for interpreting Scripture."

Norman Geisler, founder, Southern Evangelical Seminary

"It ain't the parts of the Bible that I can't understand that bother me; it is the parts that I do understand."

Mark Twain

OPTIONAL DISCUSSION QUESTIONS
for Those Investigating Christianity

- Short of seeing it with your own eyes, how can you ever really know for sure that an event actually occurred? How are you able to verify everyday occurrences without actually observing them?

- What are the pros and cons of "eyewitness testimony"? How trustworthy do you think it can ever really be? How important is it in determining the facts of any case? What factors might help you weigh whether any particular eyewitness account is accurate?

- Given your understanding of the oral tradition, how likely is it that the information and events recorded in the New Testament have been reliably preserved between the time they occurred and the time they were actually written down?

- Scholar J. P. Moreland points out that we have virtually the entire New Testament preserved in the historical quotations of the church fathers of the first four centuries, so that even if we had no copies of the New Testament, we could reconstruct it from just these quotes. How does this additional fact affect your opinion of the reliability of the New Testament document we have today?

- If the biblical authors were in collusion to create a false testimony, why do you think they didn't plan more carefully and make the incidental details of their accounts more similar? Do you agree with the supposition that if the Gospels were too consistent, that fact would invalidate them as independent witnesses? Why or why not?

Between Sessions

Personal Reflection

> *In my former book, Theophilus, I wrote about all that Jesus began to do and to teach until the day he was taken up to heaven, after giving instructions through the Holy Spirit to the apostles he had chosen. After his suffering, he presented himself to them and gave many convincing proofs that he was alive. He appeared to them over a period of forty days and spoke about the kingdom of God.*
>
> Acts 1:1–3

1. Read the above introduction to the book of Acts, written by Luke. In it, he refers to his former book, which, like Acts, was also written in the form of a letter. Does Luke seem to be sincere in his explanation for writing these letters to Theophilus? What kind of information does Luke report? Does he appear to believe his account himself? What do you suppose might be his level of concern for accuracy? Do you believe he intended to be truthful?

2. The second chapter of Luke begins:

> *In those days Caesar Augustus issued a decree that a census should be taken of the entire Roman world. (This was the first census that took place while Quirinius was governor of Syria.) And everyone went to their own town to register. So Joseph also went up from the town of Nazareth in Galilee to Judea, to Bethlehem the town of David, because he belonged to the house and line of David.*
>
> Luke 2:1–4

Does Luke include any specific details that might be verifiable two thousand years later? If so, which ones? Why do you suppose he includes this information? Are you surprised to learn that the Bible is full of such verifiable historical details? What implications would result if you learned that corroborative evidence exists to support the information that the Bible contains?

3. Consider which questions and doubts about the accuracy of the Bible have been addressed so far. What questions still remain or have arisen for you? What additional steps could you take to resolve these issues?

4. Be honest with yourself and consider how your confidence in the Bible has been affected by this session. If you remain unconvinced, what would it take to convince you that the Bible is a trustworthy historical document? And further, what would it take to convince you that the Bible is a trustworthy *spiritual* document? Would you at this moment say a short prayer and ask God to open your heart and mind to the truth about the Bible?

Personal Reading

Please read the following book content in preparation for session three:

The Case for Christ, chapter 4: The Corroborating Evidence

The Case for Christ, chapter 6: The Rebuttal Evidence

Evidence
Outside the Bible

What if there were other biographies of Jesus that have been censored because the early church didn't like the image of Jesus they portrayed? How could I have confidence that church politics haven't squelched biographies of Jesus that were every bit as accurate as the four that were finally included in the New Testament, and that would shed important new light on the words and deeds of this controversial carpenter from Nazareth?... If the Jesus of faith is not also the Jesus of history, he's powerless and he's meaningless. Unless he's rooted in reality, unless he established his divinity by rising from the dead, he's just a feel-good symbol who's as irrelevant as Santa Claus.

Lee Strobel, *The Case for Christ*

Watch This!

Video Teaching Segment

Space is provided to take notes on anything that stands out to you.

Discuss This!

1. Was Jesus a real person in history? Give a brief historical (but perhaps not spiritual) description of the general events surrounding his life and death.

"If the New Testament were a collection of secular writings, their authenticity would generally be regarded as beyond all doubt."

—Historian F. F. Bruce

FAST FACT

Corroborative Evidence

Webster's dictionary defines corroborate *this way: "To make more certain; confirm: He corroborated my account of the accident."*

Corroborative evidence supports other testimony; it affirms or backs up the essential elements of an eyewitness account. It can be a public record, a photograph, or additional testimony from a second or third person. It can verify a person's entire testimony or just key parts of it. In effect, corroborative evidence acts like the support wires that keep a tall antenna straight and unwavering. The more corroborative evidence, the stronger and more secure the case.

2. Describe an incident in which you doubted someone's story until he or she offered some corroborating evidence. What criteria helped you determine the level of relevancy of this supporting evidence?

THINK ABOUT THIS!

"Let's pretend we didn't have any of the New Testament or other Christian writings. Even without them, what would we be able to conclude about Jesus from ancient non-Christian sources, such as Josephus, the Talmud, Tacitus, Pliny the Younger, and others?"

Lee Strobel

"Often the same people, places, and events referenced inside Scripture are cited also in non-biblical materials. These range from a myriad of geographical place names to the hard evidence by archaeology to a host of documents that have come down to us from the ancient world that correlate completely with the biblical evidence."

Historian Paul Maier, Western Michigan University

"We would still have a considerable amount of important historical evidence [about Jesus without the New Testament]; in fact, it would provide a kind of outline for the life of Jesus. We would know that first, Jesus was a Jewish teacher; second, many people believed that he performed healings and exorcisms; third, some people believed he was the Messiah; fourth, he was rejected by the Jewish leaders; fifth, he was crucified under Pontius Pilate in the reign of Tiberius; sixth, despite this shameful death, his followers, who believed that he was still alive, spread beyond Palestine so that there were multitudes of them in Rome by AD 64; and seventh, all kinds of people from the cities and countryside — men and women, slave and free — worshiped him as God."

Historian Edwin M. Yamauchi, Miami (Ohio) University

"This was indeed an impressive amount of independent corroboration. And not only can the contours of Jesus' life be reconstructed apart from the Bible, but there's even more that can be gleaned about him from material so old that it actually predates the Gospels themselves."

Lee Strobel

THINK ABOUT THIS!

Josephus

"Josephus was a very important Jewish historian of the first century. He was born in AD 37, and he wrote most of his four works toward the end of the first century. He was a priest, a Pharisee, and he was somewhat egotistical. His most ambitious work was called The Antiquities, which was a history of the Jewish people from Creation until his time. He probably completed it in about AD 93."

Edwin M. Yamauchi

"He convened a meeting of the Sanhedrin and brought before them a man named James, the brother of Jesus, who was called the Christ, and certain others. He accused them of having transgressed the law and delivered them up to be stoned."

Josephus, *The Antiquities*

"Now there was about this time Jesus, a wise man, for he was a doer of wonderful works, a teacher of such men as received the truth with pleasure. He drew over to him both many of the Jews and many of the Gentiles. When Pilate, at the suggestion of the principle men amongst us, had condemned him to the cross, those that loved him first did not forsake him. And the tribe of Christians so named for him are not extinct to this day."

Josephus, *Testimonium Flavianum*

"Josephus corroborates important information about Jesus: that he was the martyred leader of the church in Jerusalem and that he was a wise teacher who had established a wide and lasting following, despite the fact that he had been crucified under Pilate at the instigation of some of the Jewish leaders. [Josephus'] accounts of the Jewish War have proved to be very accurate; for example, they've been corroborated through archaeological excavations at Masada as well as by historians like Tacitus. He's considered to be a pretty reliable historian, and his mentioning of Jesus is considered extremely important."

Edwin M. Yamauchi

3. How does the fact that the Jewish historian, Josephus, gives accurate accounts of other historical details support his accounts of Jesus and the early Christians?

Tacitus

"Tacitus recorded what is probably the most important reference to Jesus outside the New Testament. In AD 115 he explicitly states that Nero persecuted the Christians as scapegoats to divert suspicion away from himself for the great fire that had devastated Rome in AD 64."

Edwin M. Yamauchi

"Nero fastened the guilt and inflicted the most exquisite tortures on a class hated for their abominations, called Christians by the populace. Christus, from whom the name had its origin, suffered the extreme penalty during the reign of Tiberius at the hands of one of our procurators, Pontius Pilatus, and a most mischievous superstition, thus checked for the moment, again broke out not only in Judaea, the first source of the evil, but even in Rome ... Accordingly, an arrest was first made of all who pleaded guilty: then, upon their information, an immense multitude was convicted, not so much of the crime of firing the city, as of hatred against mankind."

Tacitus, *Annals*

4. How does the fact that Tacitus does not align himself with Christians affect your confidence in the reliability of his "outside" evidence for Jesus? Do you think he was trying to promote Christianity in any way? Do you think he believed that Jesus was a real historical figure?

Pliny the Younger

"[Pliny the Younger] was the nephew of Pliny the Elder, the famous encyclopedist who died in the eruption of Vesuvius in AD 79. Pliny the Younger became governor of Bithynia in northwestern Turkey. Much of his correspondence with his friend, Emperor Trajan, has been preserved to the present time."

Edwin Yamauchi

"I have asked them if they are Christians, and if they admit it, I repeat the question a second and third time, with a warning of the punishment awaiting them. If they persist, I order them to be led away for execution; for, whatever the nature of their admission, I am convinced that their stubbornness and unshakable obstinacy ought not to go unpunished ... They also declared that the sum total of their guilt or error amounted to no more than this: they had met regularly before dawn on a fixed day to chant verses alternately amongst themselves in honor of Christ as if to a god, and also to bind themselves by oath, not for any criminal purpose, but to abstain from theft, robbery, and adultery ... This made me decide it was all the more necessary to extract the truth by torture from two slave-women, whom they called deaconesses. I found nothing but a degenerate sort of cult carried to extravagant lengths."

Pliny the Younger, *Letters*

Tertullian and Phlegon

"To me, one of the most problematic references in the New Testament is where the Gospel writers claim that the earth went dark during part of the time that Jesus hung on the cross. Wasn't this merely a literary device to stress the significance of the crucifixion, and not a reference to an actual historical occurrence? After all, if darkness had fallen over the earth, wouldn't there be at least some mention of this extraordinary event outside the Bible?"

Lee Strobel

"This phenomenon, evidently, was visible in Rome, Athens, and other Mediterranean cities. According to Tertullian ... it was a 'cosmic' or 'world event.' Phlegon, a Greek author from Caria writing a chronology soon after 137 AD, reported that in the fourth year of the 202nd Olympiad (i.e., 33 AD) there was 'the greatest eclipse of the sun' and that 'it became night in the sixth hour of the day [i.e., noon] so that stars

even appeared in the heavens. There was a great earthquake in Bithynia, and many things were overturned in Nicaea.'"

Historian Paul Maier

5. Of the examples of extrabiblical writings given in this session, which ones do you consider to be the most interesting, credible, or compelling? Elaborate.

"The various Gnostic gospels were late arrivals, which is one reason why church leaders rejected them ... They lacked authority since their authors were neither (a) apostles of Jesus nor (b) persons associated with apostles of Jesus ... No one really knows who wrote the texts."

— Christian apologist Richard Abanes

6. Examine the following chart that compares some of the teachings in the most popular Gnostic text, the Gospel of Thomas, to the teachings of the New Testament. Do you see any way the teachings of Thomas can be reconciled with the biblical teachings? Why or why not?

Subject	Gospel of Thomas (written between 100 – 500 AD)	New Testament (written between 50 – 90 AD)
Who is Jesus?	Someone who imparts secret teachings to the disciples who are mature enough to receive it.	The redeemer who saves his people from sin.
Salvation	Salvation comes through a special, secret knowledge. You have to be worthy to receive that knowledge.	Salvation comes through faith in Jesus. "And you can't take credit for this; it is a gift from God" (Ephesians 2:8 NLT).
Fasting, prayer, and giving	"If you fast, you will bring sin upon yourselves, and if you pray, you will be condemned, and if you give to charity, you will harm your spirits" (Saying 14).	"When you fast, comb your hair and wash your face" (Matthew 6:17 NLT).
		"And pray in the Spirit on all occasions with all kinds of prayers and requests" (Ephesians 6:18).
		"If [your gift] is giving, then give generously" (Romans 12:8).

"Everyone who will make herself male will enter the kingdom of heaven."
— The Gospel of Thomas

THINK ABOUT THIS!

"There are no new discoveries that tell us anything new about Jesus. The Gospel of Thomas was discovered long ago, but it's only now being used to create an alternative Jesus. Some theories about the Gospel of Thomas may be new, but the gospel itself is not."

Gregory Boyd, PhD

7. The various Gnostic gospels were written sometime between the late second century and the sixth century AD, while even the most skeptical scholars concede the biblical Gospels were written in the first century, which is when Jesus lived. Jesus was executed in either AD 30 or 33. Many experts date the gospel of Mark to the late 50s or early 60s; the gospels of Matthew and Luke to the early 60s; and John to the 90s (though some argue it was written earlier). What does the dating of a gospel tell you regarding its credibility? How important is it to you that an ancient document was written close to the events it describes? How significant is it that the biblical Gospels were authored by actual apostles of Jesus or persons associated with his apostles, while the Gnostic gospels were not?

THINK ABOUT THIS!

"'More than eighty gospels were considered for the New Testament, and yet only a relative few were chosen for inclusion — Matthew, Mark, Luke, and John among them ...' Teabing located a huge book and pulled it toward him across the table. The leather-bound edition was poster-sized, like a huge atlas. The cover read: The Gnostic Gospels. Teabing heaved it open ... 'These are photocopies of ... the earliest Christian records. Troublingly, they do not match up with the gospels in the Bible ...' Flipping toward the middle of the book, Teabing pointed to a passage, 'The Gospel of Philip is always a good place to start.'"

Fictional character Sir Leigh Teabing, from *The Da Vinci Code*

"There is a view among some that there were all of these different competing views of Jesus Christ and the one that won out became the orthodox perspective of Christ reflected in the Gospels. All the evidence runs contrary to that."

New Testament scholar Mark Strauss

"Jesus is not a symbol of anything unless he's rooted in history. The Nicene Creed doesn't say, 'We wish these things were true.' It says, 'Jesus Christ was crucified under Pontius Pilate, and the third day he rose again from the dead,' and it goes on from there. The theological truth is based on historical truth. That's the way the New Testament reads. Look at the sermon of Peter in the second chapter of Acts. He stands up and says, 'You guys are a witness of these things; they weren't done in secret.'"

Gregory Boyd, PhD

8. In *The Case for Christ*, Gregory Boyd states, "I don't want to base my life on a symbol. I want reality." What do you think he means by this statement? Do you agree or disagree with his conviction? Is it enough that Jesus is a symbol of hope, or is it important for you to be confident that his life, teachings, and resurrection are rooted in history? Why?

OPTIONAL DISCUSSION QUESTIONS
for Those Investigating Christianity

- How do you evaluate and critique one biographer from another? For instance, there have been many biographers of Abraham Lincoln: Carl Sandburg, Gore Vidal, David Herbert Donald, Stephen B. Oates, and even a television documentary by Ken Burns. What are some factors that help you discern the credibility of each biography?

- What do the corroborative writings offered in this session confirm for you? What do they fail to confirm? In your opinion, which parts of Jesus' life and ministry have been corroborated?

- What do you think of this comment from Christian apologist Mark Mittelberg: "Why should the New Testament be ignored as a source for Jesus when it passes the tests of historicity? Just because certain documents are included in the Bible shouldn't automatically exclude them from consideration as if they are somehow tainted."

- In the video, Craig Evans makes the observation that people are free to "pick and choose" between two versions of Jesus. Someone may prefer the second-century Gnostic Jesus better, while others might like the early first-century Palestinian Jesus. Do you think preferences or feelings are a good way to decide what to believe? Why or why not?

- Often, scholars are accused of finding the Jesus they wanted to find. Said Charlotte Allen in *The Human Christ*: "The liberal searchers found a liberal Jesus, the deists found a deist, the Romantics a Romantic, the existentialists an existentialist, and the liberationists a Jesus of class struggle." Is it possible to find the *real* Jesus? What are some ways we can safeguard against our natural tendency to make Jesus fit into our preconceptions or personal tastes?

Between Sessions

Personal Reflection

"LORD, who may dwell in your sacred tent? Who may live on your holy mountain? The one whose walk is blameless, who does what is righteous, who speaks the truth from their heart."

Psalm 15:1–2

"Guide me in your truth and teach me, for you are God my Savior, and my hope is in you all day long."

Psalm 25:5

"Do not withhold your mercy from me, LORD; may your love and your truth always protect me."

Psalm 40:11

"Yet you desire faithfulness even in the womb; you taught me wisdom in that secret place."

Psalm 51:6

"The LORD is near to all who call on him, to all who call on him in truth."

Psalm 145:18

"Then you will know the truth, and the truth will set you free."

John 8:32

1. What determines for you what you believe to be true? Are you a "facts and data" person or do you rely more on gut feelings? Can you think of an example of a time when a gut feeling you had proved to be true? How about a time when something you were absolutely sure of proved not to be true? How willing were you to change your mental paradigm once the facts were presented?

2. What about evidence? To what extent do you genuinely examine the evidence for any given story? Are you the type that goes to *snopes.com* when a questionable email arrives? Or are you someone who considers the source of the email and lets your opinion of the sender affect your opinion of the content? Which is most important to you: to learn the truth even when it contradicts your current belief system or to believe in something that may be false, but is comfortable?

3. How important is truth to you? According to the verses on the previous page, what value do the authors of the Bible place on truth? What value do you think Jesus placed on truth? How hard are you willing to search for the truth about Jesus?

4. Some would say that the story of Jesus Christ is a feel-good story that is too good to be true. Others would say there are no facts to support it and that Jesus was a mythological figure who never even existed. Many think the Bible is unreliable and the events it contains are spurious and uncorroborated by history. Is this what you have believed in the past? Is this an accurate reflection of what you believe now? Is this what the evidence supports?

5. What have you learned in this discussion or in your reading that has challenged your current belief system? How open are you to assimilating this new information? As Psalm 145:18 says, "The LORD is near all who call on him, to all who call on him in truth." Are you willing to call on the Lord right now and disclose your beliefs, doubts, and concerns? If you do, he promises to be near you and to hear you. He is listening.

Personal Reading

Please read the following book content in preparation for session four:

The Case for Christ, chapter 9: The Profile Evidence

The Case for Christ, chapter 10: The Fingerprint Evidence

Analyzing Jesus

As far as I was concerned, the case was closed. There was enough proof for me to rest easy with the conclusion that the divinity of Jesus was nothing more than the fanciful invention of superstitious people ... Frankly, I had wanted to believe that the deification of Jesus was the result of legendary development in which well-meaning but misguided people slowly turned a wise sage into the mythological Son of God. That seemed safe and reassuring; after all, a roving apocalyptic preacher from the first century could make no demands on me. But while I went into my investigation thinking that this legendary explanation was intuitively obvious, I emerged convinced it was totally without basis.

Lee Strobel, *The Case for Christ*

Watch This!

Video Teaching Segment

Space is provided to take notes on anything that stands out to you.

Discuss This!

1. Define "miracle." What is the difference between a miracle and a magic trick? Are real miracles possible?

2. Craig Evans points out that Jesus' contemporaries — that is, people who liked him, people who were indifferent, and people who opposed him — all acknowledged that Jesus did extraordinary things. What about you? Do you think Jesus really performed miracles such as commanding nature, healing the sick, and raising the dead? Elaborate.

"Jesus' biggest distinctive is how he did miracles on his own authority. He is the one who says, 'If I, by the finger of God, cast out demons, then the kingdom of God is among you' — he's referring to himself. He says, 'I have been anointed to set the captives free.' He does give God the Father credit for what he does, but you never find him asking God the Father to do it — he does it in the power of God the Father. And for that there is just no parallel."
— Gregory Boyd, PhD

THINK ABOUT THIS!

Now while he was in Jerusalem at the Passover Festival, many people saw the signs [miracles] he was performing and believed in his name.

John 2:23

The Jews who were there gathered around him, saying, "How long will you keep us in suspense? If you are the Messiah, tell us plainly." Jesus answered, "I did tell you, but you do not believe. The works [miracles] I do in my Father's name testify about me."

John 10:24–25

cont.

> But when the Pharisees heard this, they said, "It is only by Beelzebul, the prince of demons, that this fellow drives out demons."
>
> Matthew 12:24

3. During the time Jesus was performing miracles, people who believed in him were convinced he was filled with the Spirit of God, while those who opposed him were convinced he was of the devil. What do you think was the power source behind his miraculous acts? Elaborate. What are some factors that would delineate between a good power source and an evil power source?

4. What do you think was the significance or ultimate purpose of Jesus' miracles?

For in Christ all the
fullness of the Deity
lives in bodily form.
(Colossians 2:9)

THINK ABOUT THIS!

Knowing their thoughts, Jesus said, "Why do you entertain evil thoughts in your hearts? Which is easier: to say, 'Your sins are forgiven,' or to say, 'Get up and walk'? But I want you to know that the Son of Man has authority on earth to forgive sins." So he said to the paralyzed man, "Get up, take your mat and go home."

Matthew 9:4 – 6

5. In the video Mark Strauss suggests that the most astonishing thing Jesus did was claim to be able to forgive sins. Why is this claim so remarkable? Do you really believe Jesus has the power to forgive sins? Describe what it would feel like for you personally if you could have your slate wiped clean and every wrong you've ever done completely forgiven.

6. Strauss further explains that Jesus' miracles confirmed that he in fact did have the power and authority to forgive sins. Do you agree or disagree with Strauss's logic? Explain.

"When David sinned by committing adultery and arranging the death of the woman's husband, he ultimately says to God in Psalm 51, 'Against you only have I sinned and done this evil in your sight.' He recognized that although he had wronged people, in the end he had sinned against the God who made him in his image, and God needed to forgive him. So along comes Jesus and says to sinners, 'I forgive you.' The Jews immediately recognize the blasphemy of this. They react by saying, 'Who can forgive sins but God alone?' To my mind, that is one of the most striking things Jesus did."

New Testament scholar Donald A. Carson

FAST FACT

Messiah, in Hebrew, means "the promised and expected deliverer." When the term is used in the Old Testament, it specifically pertains to the Jewish people. The Greek word for "Messiah" is "Christ." In the New Testament the Christ is revealed to be the anointed one and the deliverer who has come for all who would receive him.

7. Where did the idea of a Messiah come from? How and why did the Jews expect to receive a Messiah? To what degree are you looking for a Messiah in your own life?

[Jesus] said to them, "This is what I told you while I was still with you: Everything must be fulfilled that is written about me in the Law of Moses, the Prophets and the Psalms."

(Luke 24:44)

THINK ABOUT THIS!

"The premise behind fingerprint evidence is simple: each individual has unique ridges on his or her fingers. When a print found on an object matches the pattern of ridges on a person's finger, investigators can conclude with scientific certainty that this specific individual has touched that object… There is another kind of evidence that's analogous to fingerprints and establishes to an astounding degree of certainty that Jesus is indeed the Messiah of Israel and the world. In the Jewish Scriptures, which Christians call the Old Testament, there are several dozen major prophecies about the coming of the Messiah, who would be sent by God to redeem his people. In effect, these predictions formed a figurative fingerprint that only the Anointed One would be able to match. This way, the Israelites could rule out any impostors and validate the credentials of the authentic Messiah. The Greek word for "Messiah" is Christ. But was Jesus really the Christ? Did he miraculously fulfill these predictions that were written hundreds of years before he was born? And how do we know he was the only individual throughout history who fit the prophetic fingerprint?"

Lee Strobel

Fulfilled Prophecy	Old Testament Reference	Approx. Years Written before Jesus
He would be born of a virgin.	Isaiah 7:14	700
He would be born in Bethlehem.	Micah 5:2	700
He would be mocked and scorned, whipped, and killed by the piercing of his hands and feet. His bones would be out of joint; his garments would be divided by the casting of lots (dice).	Psalm 22	300 – 1,000
The time of his birth was predicted.	Daniel 9:24 – 26	600
He would come from the seed of a woman.	Genesis 3:15	1,400
He would be a descendant of Abraham, Isaac, Jacob, and David.	Genesis 12:3; 17:19 Numbers 24:17 Isaiah 9:7	700 – 1,400

cont.

Fulfilled Prophecy	Old Testament Reference	Approx. Years Written before Jesus
He would come from the tribe of Judah.	Genesis 49:10	1,400
He would heal the deaf and blind.	Isaiah 29:18	700
He would be rejected by his own people, the Jews.	Isaiah 53:3	700
He would teach with parables.	Psalm 78:2	300 – 1,000
Kings and rulers would plot to kill him.	Psalm 2:2	300 – 1,000
He would be betrayed by a close friend.	Psalm 41:9	300 – 1,000
He would be betrayed for thirty pieces of silver.	Zechariah 11:12	500
His disciples would be scattered.	Zechariah 13:7	500
His bones would remain unbroken.	Psalm 34:20	300 – 1,000
He would be buried in a rich man's grave.	Isaiah 53:9	700
He would be resurrected on the third day.	Psalm 16:10 Hosea 6:2	300 – 1,000

"The Old Testament paints a portrait of God by using such titles and descriptions as Alpha and Omega, Lord, Savior, King, Judge, Light, Rock, Redeemer, Shepherd, Creator, giver of life, forgiver of sin, and speaker with divine authority. It's fascinating to note that in the New Testament each and every one is applied to Jesus. Jesus said it all in John 14:7: 'If you really knew me, you would know my Father as well.' Loose translation: 'When you look at the sketch of God from the Old Testament, you will see a likeness of me.'"

— Lee Strobel

8. What's your overall reaction or response to the detailed list of the messianic prophecies found in the Bible? What questions or issues does this subject matter raise in your mind?

THINK ABOUT THIS!

Consider the following words from the Jewish prophet Isaiah, written approximately seven hundred years before Jesus lived:

> *He was despised and rejected by mankind, a man of suffering, and familiar with pain. Like one from whom people hide their faces he was despised, and we held him in low esteem. Surely he took up our pain and bore our suffering, yet we considered him punished by God, stricken by him, and afflicted. But he was pierced for our transgressions, he was crushed for our iniquities; the punishment that brought us peace was on him, and by his wounds we are healed. We all, like sheep, have gone astray, each of us has turned to our own way; and*

*the LORD has laid on him the iniquity of us all. He was oppressed and
afflicted, yet he did not open his mouth; he was led like a lamb to the
slaughter, and as a sheep before its shearers is silent, so he did not open
his mouth. By oppression and judgment he was taken away. Yet who of
his generation protested? For he was cut off from the land of the living;
for the transgression of my people he was punished. He was assigned
a grave with the wicked, and with the rich in his death, though he
had done no violence, nor was any deceit in his mouth ... Therefore I
will give him a portion among the great, and he will divide the spoils
with the strong, because he poured out his life unto death, and was
numbered with the transgressors. For he bore the sin of many, and
made intercession for the transgressors.*

Isaiah 53:3 – 9, 12

"[In Isaiah 53] it's almost as if God said, 'I want to make it so absolutely clear Yeshua
[Jesus] is the Messiah that it's undeniable.' I almost feel as if God would have to
apologize to the human race and to the Jewish people for putting this passage into
the Scriptures when it so clearly points to Yeshua if he didn't really mean that."

Prophecy scholar Michael L. Brown

"For a few of the prophecies, yes, that's certainly conceivable that Jesus could have
intentionally fulfilled them, as some claim. But there are many others for which this
just wouldn't have been possible. For instance, how would he control the fact that
the Sanhedrin offered Judas thirty pieces of silver to betray him? How could he arrange for his ancestry, or to be born when and where he was, or his method of execution, or that soldiers gambled for his clothing, or that his legs remained unbroken on
the cross? How would he arrange to perform miracles in front of skeptics? How would
he arrange for his resurrection? When you interpret Daniel 9:24 – 26, it foretells that
the Messiah would appear a certain length of time after King Artaxerxes issued a
decree for the Jewish people to go from Persia to rebuild the walls in Jerusalem. That
puts the anticipated appearance of the Messiah at the exact moment in history
when Jesus showed up. Certainly that's nothing he could have prearranged."

Prophecies scholar Louis Lapides

9. How does the fulfillment of the Old Testament prophecies by Jesus relate to his identity, namely his divinity?

"A college professor of mathematics and science named Dr. Peter Stoner wanted to determine what the odds were that any human being throughout human history could fulfill the messianic prophecies. He estimated that the odds of any human being fulfilling 48 of these ancient prophecies would be one chance in a trillion, trillion, trillion, trillion, trillion, trillion, trillion, trillion, trillion, trillion, trillion, trillion, trillion."

Lee Strobel

"I think it would be mathematically impossible for anyone else ever to fulfill all these parameters of prophecy in the Old Testament any better than Jesus did."

Ancient historian Paul Maier, Western Michigan University

"All the evidence points to Jesus as the divinely appointed fulfillment of the messianic prophecies. He was God's man, confirmed by God's signs."

Scholar Norman Geisler

cont.

"Jesus is the right continuation of my Jewish roots. He's the Messiah of Israel and the savior of the world … So really he is the ultimate expression of God to the human race. That's why I'm spending my life talking to Jewish people — as compassionately and accurately as I can — about the reality of Jesus the Messiah. I just can't withhold God's very best from those he dearly loves."

Prophecies scholar Michael L. Brown

10. How convinced are you that Jesus — and Jesus alone — fulfills the Old Testament prophecies for the Messiah? What are the implications for all of humanity if Jesus really was God in the flesh? What are the implications for *your* life if Jesus really was God in the flesh? What is a difficult or troublesome aspect of this truth for your life today?

OPTIONAL DISCUSSION QUESTIONS
for Those Investigating Christianity

- Which of the following attributes of Jesus would you consider to be strong evidence for the divinity of Jesus?

  – He claimed to forgive sins. (Mark 2:1–12; Luke 5:17–26; 7:36–50)

  – He accepted worship. (Matthew 14:33; 28:9, 17; Luke 24:52; John 9:38)

  – He exorcized demons. (Matthew 8:28–34; Mark 1:34, 39; 9:14–29)

  – He demonstrated control over the elements. (Matthew 8:23–27; Mark 4:35–41; John 2:1–11)

  – He healed the sick. (Matthew 4:23; 8:1–13; 9:1–8, 18–34; Mark 1:34; Luke 8:40–48; John 9:1–7)

  – He had authority over life and death. (Mark 5:21–43; Luke 8:49–56; John 11:1–44)

  – He was said to be without sin. (1 Peter 2:22; 1 John 3:5)

- To what extent has the information presented and discussed in this session influenced your opinion of the identity of Jesus Christ? What aspect of Jesus' divinity is troublesome or difficult for you to accept? Why?

- How convinced are you that Jesus is the Messiah, the Christ, the Anointed One, the One sent by God to be the Savior of Israel and the world. What anxieties do you have about believing this? How would your friends and family members react? Do you see any costs that you might incur if you were to become a Christian? How might those costs compare with the benefits?

Between Sessions

Personal Reflection

When one of the Pharisees invited Jesus to have dinner with him, he went to the Pharisee's house and reclined at the table. A woman in that town who lived a sinful life learned that Jesus was eating at the Pharisee's house, so she came there with an alabaster jar of perfume. As she stood behind him at his feet weeping, she began to wet his feet with her tears. Then she wiped them with her hair, kissed them and poured perfume on them.

When the Pharisee who had invited him saw this, he said to himself, "If this man were a prophet, he would know who is touching him and what kind of woman she is — that she is a sinner." Jesus answered him, "Simon, I have something to tell you." "Tell me, teacher," he said.

"Two people owed money to a certain moneylender. One owed him five hundred denarii, and the other fifty. Neither of them had the money to pay him back, so he forgave the debts of both. Now which of them will love him more?" Simon replied, "I suppose the one who had the bigger debt forgiven." "You have judged correctly," Jesus said.

Then he turned toward the woman and said to Simon, "Do you see this woman? I came into your house. You did not give me any water for my feet, but she wet my feet with her tears and wiped them with her hair. You did not give me a kiss, but this woman, from the time I entered, has not stopped kissing my feet. You did not put oil on my head, but she has poured perfume on my feet. Therefore, I tell you, her many sins have been forgiven — as her great love has shown. But whoever has been forgiven little loves little." Then Jesus said to her, "Your sins are forgiven." The other guests began to say among themselves, "Who is this who even forgives sins?" Jesus said to the woman, "Your faith has saved you; go in peace."

Luke 7:36–50

1. Think about your own sins and shortfalls. If you are willing, think about the most shameful things you have ever done. Remember the lying, the cheating, the stealing, the lusting, the times you put things or people before God? When Jesus walked this earth, he claimed to be able to forgive even the worst sins of all those who repented and had faith

in him. In his death he paid the price for the sins of all humankind —
including yours. Can a mere human being actually forgive everything
you have ever done wrong, much less take the punishment for the sins
of all humankind? This is what Jesus claimed to do. What do you make
of Jesus' claims?

2. If Jesus is divine and has the authority to forgive sin, what does this
   mean for you personally? How miraculous would it be for you to have
   your lifetime's accumulation of mistakes and failures completely forgiven and forever forgotten?

3. Consider the woman in the account from Luke 7. What do you think led her to worship and love Jesus as she did? Is there anything that could lead you to love him with such abandon?

4. The Bible teaches that if we confess, repent (turn away from our sin), and ask for forgiveness, we will be totally forgiven and received into the family of God. If you have never asked for God's forgiveness, you can do so anywhere at any time with a simple, heartfelt prayer. When you turn to him in genuine faith, he promises that absolutely nothing will keep him from coming to you. Jesus himself said, "Come to me, all you who are weary and burdened, and I will give you rest. Take my yoke upon you and learn from me, for I am gentle and humble in heart, and you will find rest for your souls" (Matthew 11:28–29). Thank him for his forgiveness.

Personal Reading

Please read the following book content in preparation for session five:

The Case for Christ, chapter 11: The Medical Evidence

The Case for Christ, chapter 12: The Evidence of the Missing Body

The Case for Christ, chapter 13: The Evidence of Appearances

Evidence
for the Resurrection

Occasionally bodies turn up missing in pulp fiction and real life, but rarely do you encounter an empty tomb ... The issue with Jesus isn't that he was nowhere to be seen. It's that he was seen, alive; he was seen, dead; and he was seen, alive once more. If we believe the Gospel accounts, this isn't a matter of a missing body. No, it's a matter of Jesus still being alive, even to this day, even after publicly succumbing to the horrors of crucifixion.

Lee Strobel, *The Case for Christ*

Watch This!

Video Teaching Segment

Space is provided to take notes on anything that stands out to you.

Discuss This!

1. Consider the following deduction: *If it can be shown that Jesus really did return from the dead, then it can be concluded that Jesus really is who he claimed to be: the one and only Son of God.* Do you agree or disagree? Would verification of the resurrection convince you of Jesus' divinity? Explain.

"The chances of surviving the crucifixion were extremely bleak. Crucifixion and the tortures that normally preceded it was the worst way to die in antiquity. A person was scourged to the point usually that their intestines, arteries and veins were laid bare. And then after that a person was dragged out where they were impaled to a cross or a tree. And then left hanging there in excruciating pain."

— Resurrection expert Michael Licona

2. Some skeptics claim that although Jesus might have been crucified, he never really died. Instead, he merely fainted on the cross or was drugged, and later escaped as part of a conspiracy. To what extent do you think the "swoon hypothesis" (see the "Think About This!" box) makes sense? Give reasons for your explanation.

THINK ABOUT THIS!

The Swoon Hypothesis

The idea that Jesus never really died on the cross can be found in the Koran, which was written in the seventh century — in fact, Ahmadiya Muslims contend that Jesus actually fled to India. To this day there's a shrine that allegedly marks his real burial place in Srinagar, Kashmir.

As the nineteenth century dawned, Karl Bahrdt, Karl Venturini, and others tried to explain away the resurrection by suggesting that Jesus only fainted from exhaustion on the cross, or he had been given a drug that made him appear to die, and that he had later been revived by the cool, damp air of the tomb.

Conspiracy theorists bolstered this hypothesis by pointing out that Jesus had been given some liquid on a sponge while on the cross (Mark 15:36) and that Pilate seemed surprised at how quickly Jesus had succumbed (Mark 15:44). Consequently, they said, Jesus' reappearance wasn't a miraculous resurrection but merely a fortuitous resuscitation, and his tomb was empty because he continued to live.

Like an urban myth, the swoon theory continues to flourish. But what does the evidence really establish? What actually happened at the crucifixion? What was Jesus' cause of death? Is there any possible way he could have survived this ordeal?

3. Which piece of medical evidence (see the "Think About This!" boxes that follow) most stands out to you as substantiating evidence for the

biblical account of the crucifixion and death of Jesus? Which is the weakest piece of evidence or makes the least amount of sense? In your opinion, what are the odds that Jesus really survived his crucifixion? Do you think it's possible that Jesus didn't actually die on the cross and his "resurrection" was only a near-death experience from which he recovered? Give reasons for your answers.

"The pain was absolutely unbearable. In fact, it was literally beyond words to describe; they had to invent a new word: excruciating. Literally, excruciating means 'out of the cross.' Think of that: they needed to create a new word, because there was nothing in the language that could describe the intense anguish caused during the crucifixion."

— Alexander Metherell, MD, PhD

THINK ABOUT THIS!

Medical Evidence

Medical evidence can be crucial. It can determine whether a child died of abuse or an accidental fall. It can establish whether a person succumbed to natural causes or was murdered by someone who spiked the person's coffee with arsenic. It can uphold or dismantle a defendant's alibi by pinpointing the victim's time of death, using an ingenious procedure that measures the amount of potassium in the eyes of the deceased. And yes, even in the case of someone brutally executed on a Roman cross two millennia ago, medical evidence can still make a crucial contribution: it can destroy one of the most persistent arguments used by those who claim that the resurrection of Jesus — the supreme vindication of his claim to deity — was nothing more than an elaborate hoax.

Jesus Is Flogged

Then Pilate took Jesus and had him flogged. The soldiers twisted together a crown of thorns and put it on his head. They clothed him in a purple robe and went up to him again and again, saying, "Hail, king of the Jews!" And they slapped him in the face.

John 19:1 – 3

Then the governor's soldiers took Jesus into the Praetorium and gathered the whole company of soldiers around him. They stripped him and put a scarlet robe on him, and then twisted together a crown of thorns and set it on his head. They put a staff in his right hand. Then they knelt in front of him and mocked him. "Hail, king of the Jews!" they said. They spit on him, and took the staff and struck him on the head again and again. After they had mocked him, they took off the robe and put his own clothes on him. Then they led him away to crucify him.

Matthew 27:27 – 31

Roman Floggings

"Roman floggings were known to be terribly brutal. They usually consisted of thirty-nine lashes. The soldier would use a whip of braided leather thongs with metal balls woven into them. When the whip would strike the flesh, these balls would cause deep bruises or contusions, which would break open with further blows. And the whip had pieces of sharp bone as well, which would cut the flesh severely. One physician who has studied Roman beatings said, 'As the flogging continued, the lacerations would tear into the underlying skeletal muscles and produce quivering ribbons of bleeding flesh.' A third-century historian by the name of Eusebius described a flogging by saying, 'The sufferer's veins were laid bare, and the very muscles, sinews, and bowels of the victim were open to exposure.' We know that many people would die from this kind of beating even before they could be crucified. At the least, the victim would experience tremendous pain and go into hypovolemic shock."

Alexander Metherell

FAST FACT

Hypovolemic shock: Hypo *means "low,"* vol *refers to volume, and* emic *means "blood," so hypovolemic shock means the person is suffering the effects of losing a large amount of blood. This does four things. First, the heart races to try to pump blood that isn't there; second, the blood pressure drops, causing fainting or collapse; third, the kidneys stop producing urine to maintain what volume is left; and fourth, the person becomes very thirsty as the body craves fluids to replace the lost blood volume.*

THINK ABOUT THIS!

Jesus Is Crucified

So the soldiers took charge of Jesus. Carrying his own cross, he went out to the place of the Skull (which in Aramaic is called Golgotha). There they crucified him, and with him two others — one on each side and Jesus in the middle. Pilate had a notice prepared and fastened to the cross. It read: JESUS OF NAZARETH, THE KING OF THE JEWS. Many of the Jews read this sign, for the place where Jesus was crucified was near the city, and the sign was written in Aramaic, Latin and Greek. The chief priests of the Jews protested to Pilate, "Do not write 'The King of the Jews,' but that this man claimed to be king of the Jews." Pilate answered, "What I have written, I have written." When the soldiers crucified Jesus, they took his clothes, dividing them into four shares, one for each of them, with the undergarment remaining. This garment was seamless, woven in one piece from top to bottom. "Let's not tear it," they said to one another. "Let's decide by lot who will get it." This happened that the scripture might be fulfilled that said, "They divided my clothes among them and cast lots for my garment." So this is what the soldiers did.

John 19:16b – 24

Those who passed by hurled insults at him, shaking their heads and saying, "So! You who are going to destroy the temple and build it in three days, come down from the cross and save yourself!" In the same way the chief priests and the teachers of the law mocked him among themselves. "He saved others," they said, "but he can't save himself! Let this Messiah, this king of Israel, come down now from the cross, that we may see and believe." Those crucified with him also heaped insults on him.

Mark 15:29 – 32

Later, knowing that everything had now been finished, and so that Scripture would be fulfilled, Jesus said, "I am thirsty." A jar of wine vinegar was there, so they soaked a sponge in it, put the sponge on a stalk of the hyssop plant, and lifted it to Jesus' lips. When he had received the drink, Jesus said, "It is finished." With that, he bowed his head and gave up his spirit.

John 19:28 – 30

Death by Asphyxiation

"Once a person is hanging in the vertical position, crucifixion is essentially an agonizingly slow death by asphyxiation. The reason is that the stresses on the muscles and diaphragm put the chest into the inhaled position; basically, in order to exhale, the individual must push up on his feet so the tension on the muscles would be eased for a moment. In doing so, the nail would tear through the foot, eventually locking up against the tarsal bones. After managing to exhale, the person would then be able to relax down and take another breath in. Again he'd have to push himself up to exhale, scraping his bloodied back against the coarse wood of the cross. This would go on and on until complete exhaustion would take over, and the person wouldn't be able to push up and breathe anymore."

Alexander Metherell

4. Did you know that Jesus was so anguished in the garden that his sweat became like drops of blood? (See the following "Think About This!" box.) How surprised are you to learn that blood in the sweat glands is an actual medical condition due to high levels of stress? How does this medical fact affect the credibility of the biblical account? What do you think was the cause of Jesus' anguish and stress in the garden?

THINK ABOUT THIS!

Jesus Sweats Blood

Jesus went out as usual to the Mount of Olives, and his disciples followed him. On reaching the place, he said to them, "Pray that you will not fall into temptation." He withdrew about a stone's throw beyond them, knelt down and prayed, "Father, if you are willing, take this cup from me; yet not my will, but yours be done." An angel from heaven appeared to him and strengthened him. And being in anguish, he prayed more earnestly, and his sweat was like drops of blood falling to the ground.

Luke 22:39 – 44

FAST FACT

Hematidrosis: "[Hematidrosis is] not very common, but it is associated with a high degree of psychological stress. What happens is that severe anxiety causes the release of chemicals that break down the capillaries in the sweat glands. As a result, there's a small amount of bleeding into these glands, and the sweat comes out tinged with blood. We're not talking about a lot of blood; it's just a very, very small amount."

Alexander Metherell

5. In John's account of the death of Jesus, he gives a seemingly irrelevant, secondary detail that when the soldier pierced Jesus' side to be sure he was dead, both water and blood came out. (See the following "Think About This!" box.) Given that there was no medical knowledge of the conditions known as pericardial effusion (water around the heart) or pleural effusion (water around the lungs) at that time, what significance does this detail add to the credibility and accuracy of John's account?

Pierced but Not Broken

Now it was the day of Preparation, and the next day was to be a special Sabbath. Because the Jewish leaders did not want the bodies left on the crosses during the Sabbath, they asked Pilate to have the legs broken and the bodies taken down. The soldiers therefore came and broke the legs of the first man who had been crucified with Jesus, and then those of the other. But when they came to Jesus and found that he was already dead, they did not break his legs. Instead, one of the soldiers pierced Jesus' side with a spear, bringing a sudden flow of blood and water. The man who saw it has given testimony, and his testimony is true. He knows that he tells the truth, and he testifies so that you also may believe. These things happened so that the scripture would be fulfilled: "Not one of his bones will be broken," and, as another scripture says, "They will look on the one they have pierced."

John 19:31 – 37

FAST FACT

Pericardial and pleural effusion: *"Even before he died — and this is important, too — the hypovolemic shock would have caused a sustained rapid heart rate that would have contributed to heart failure, resulting in the collection of fluid in the membrane around the heart, called a pericardial effusion, as well as around the lungs, which is called a pleural effusion ... [T]he Roman soldier came around and, being fairly certain that Jesus was dead, confirmed it by thrusting a spear into his right side. The spear apparently went through the right lung and into the heart, so when the spear was pulled out, some fluid — the pericardial effusion and the pleural effusion — came out. This would have the appearance of a clear fluid, like water, followed by a large volume of blood, as the eyewitness John described in his Gospel. John probably had no idea why he saw both blood and a clear fluid come out — certainly that's not what an untrained person like him would have antici- pated. Yet John's description is consistent with what modern medicine would expect to have happened. I'll grant you that the soldiers didn't go to medical school. But remember that they were experts in killing people — that was their job, and they did it very well. They knew without a doubt when a person was dead, and really it's not so terribly difficult to figure out. Besides, if a prisoner somehow escaped, the responsible soldiers would be put to death themselves, so they had a huge incentive to make absolutely sure that each and every victim was dead when he was removed from the cross."*

Alexander Metherell

9. Read the accounts of the burial and the discovery of the empty tomb. (See the following "Think About This!" box.) What questions do they raise or answer for you? Some skeptics suggest that if Jesus was really dead and buried, then the idea of an empty tomb is impossible. So they conclude that either Jesus never really died or the tomb was never found empty. What do you think? Was the tomb really found empty? Why or why not?

"When we turn to the Gospels, we find multiple, independent attestation of this burial story, and Joseph of Arimathea is specifically named in all four accounts. On top of that, the burial story in Mark is so extremely early that it's simply not possible for it to have been subject to legendary corruption. When you read the New Testament, there's no doubt that the disciples sincerely believed the truth of the resurrection, which they proclaimed to their deaths. The idea that the empty tomb is the result of some hoax, conspiracy, or theft is simply dismissed today."

— William Lane Craig

The Burial

As evening approached, there came a rich man from Arimathea, named Joseph, who had himself become a disciple of Jesus. Going to Pilate, he asked for Jesus' body, and Pilate ordered that it be given to him. Joseph took the body, wrapped it in a clean linen cloth, and placed it in his own new tomb that he had cut out of the rock. He rolled a big stone in front of the entrance to the tomb and went away. Mary Magdalene and the other Mary were sitting there opposite the tomb. The next day, the one after Preparation Day, the chief priests and the Pharisees went to Pilate. "Sir," they said, "we remember that while he was still alive that deceiver said, 'After three days I will rise again.' So give the order for the tomb to be made secure until the third day. Otherwise, his disciples may come and steal the body and tell the people that he has been raised from the dead. This last deception will be worse than the first." "Take a guard," Pilate answered. "Go, make the tomb as secure as you know how." So they went and made the tomb secure by putting a seal on the stone and posting the guard.

Matthew 27:57 – 66

The Tomb

"There was a slanted groove that led down to a low entrance, and a large disk-shaped stone was rolled down this groove and lodged into place across the door. A smaller stone was then used to secure the disk. Although it would be easy to roll this big disk down the groove, it would take several men to roll the stone back up in order to reopen the tomb. In that sense it was quite secure."

William Lane Craig

The Empty Tomb

After the Sabbath, at dawn on the first day of the week, Mary Magdalene and the other Mary went to look at the tomb. There was a violent earthquake, for an angel of the Lord came down from heaven and, going to the tomb, rolled back the stone and sat on it. His appearance was like lightning, and his clothes were white as snow. The guards were so afraid of him that they shook and became like dead men.

The angel said to the women, "Do not be afraid, for I know that you are looking for Jesus, who was crucified. He is not here; he has risen, just as he said. Come and see the place where he lay. Then go quickly and tell his disciples: 'He has risen from the dead and is going ahead of you into Galilee. There you will see him.' Now I have told you."

So the women hurried away from the tomb, afraid yet filled with joy, and ran to tell his disciples. Suddenly Jesus met them. "Greetings," he said. They came to him, clasped his feet and worshiped him. Then Jesus said to them, "Do not be afraid. Go and tell my brothers to go to Galilee; there they will see me."

While the women were on their way, some of the guards went into the city and reported to the chief priests everything that had happened. When the chief priests had met with the elders and devised a plan, they gave the soldiers a large sum of money, telling them, "You are to say, 'His disciples came during the night and stole him away while we were asleep.' If this report gets to the governor, we will satisfy him and keep you out of trouble." So the soldiers took the money and did as they were instructed. And this story has been widely circulated among the Jews to this very day.

Matthew 28:1 – 15

7. William Lane Craig, N. T. Wright, and Michael Licona contend that if the empty tomb story were fabricated by Jesus' disciples, they never would have said that its discovery was made by women, due to women's low status in that day. (See the "Think About This!" box on the following page.) Does this argument make sense to you? Do you agree with it? Why or why not?

THINK ABOUT THIS!

Jesus Is Risen

Now Mary stood outside the tomb crying. As she wept, she bent over to look into the tomb and saw two angels in white, seated where Jesus' body had been, one at the head and the other at the foot. They asked her, "Woman, why are you crying?" "They have taken my Lord away," she said, "and I don't know where they have put him." At this, she turned around and saw Jesus standing there, but she did not realize that it was Jesus. He asked her, "Woman, why are you crying? Who is it you are looking for?" Thinking he was the gardener, she said, "Sir, if you have carried him away, tell me where you have put him, and I will get him." Jesus said to her, "Mary." She turned toward him and cried out in Aramaic, "Rabboni!" (which means "Teacher"). Jesus said, "Do not hold on to me, for I have not yet ascended to the Father. Go instead to my brothers and tell them, 'I am ascending to my Father and your Father, to my God and your God.'" Mary Magdalene went to the disciples with the news: "I have seen the Lord!" And she told them that he had said these things to her.

John 20:11 – 18

"When you understand the role of women in first-century Jewish society, what's really extraordinary is that this empty tomb story should feature women as the discoverers of the empty tomb in the first place. Women were on a very low rung of the social ladder in first-century Palestine. There are old rabbinical sayings that said, 'Let the words of the Law be burned rather than delivered to women' and 'Blessed is he whose children are male, but woe to him whose children are female.' In light of this, it's absolutely remarkable that the chief witnesses to the empty tomb are these women who were friends of Jesus. Any later legendary account would have certainly portrayed male disciples as discovering the tomb — Peter or John, for example. The fact that women are the first witnesses to the empty tomb is most plausibly explained by the reality that — like it or not — they were the discoverers of the empty tomb! This shows that the Gospel writers faithfully recorded what happened, even if it was embarrassing. This bespeaks the historicity of this tradition rather than its legendary status."

William Lane Craig

8. The creed in 1 Corinthians 15 (see the "Think About This!" box below) is the only place in ancient literature where it is claimed that Jesus appeared to five hundred people at once. The Gospels don't mention it. No secular historian mentions it. Do you agree with the reasons historian Gary Habermas gives that this creed is the earliest and one of the best authenticated passages in Scripture? Why or why not? How pivotal is this creed to your assessment of whether Jesus was seen alive after the crucifixion?

THINK ABOUT THIS!

The Earliest Christian Creed

For what I received I passed on to you as of first importance: that Christ died for our sins according to the Scriptures, that he was buried, that he was raised on the third day according to the Scriptures, and that he appeared to Cephas [Peter], and then to the Twelve. After that, he appeared to more than five hundred of the brothers and sisters at the same time, most of whom are still living, though some have fallen asleep. Then he appeared to James, then to all the apostles.

1 Corinthians 15:3 – 7

"We know that Paul wrote 1 Corinthians between AD 55 and 57. He indicates in 1 Corinthians 15:1 – 4 that he has already passed on this creed to the church at Corinth, which would mean it must predate his visit there in AD 51. Therefore the creed was being used within twenty years of the resurrection, which is quite early.

cont.

However, I'd agree with the various scholars who trace it back even further, to within two to eight years of the resurrection, or from about AD 32 to 38, when Paul received it in either Damascus or Jerusalem. So this is incredibly early material — primitive, unadorned testimony to the fact that Jesus appeared alive to skeptics like Paul and James, as well as to Peter and the rest of the disciples.

"Now, stop and think about it: you would never include this phrase [the 500] unless you were absolutely confident that these folks would confirm that they really did see Jesus alive. I mean, Paul was virtually inviting people to check it out for themselves! He wouldn't have said this if he didn't know they'd back him up. Look, I'd love to have five sources for this. I don't. But I do have one excellent source — a creed that's so good that German historian Hans von Campenhausen says, 'This account meets all the demands of historical reliability that could possibly be made of such a text.' The creed is early ... it's free from legendary contamination, ... it's unambiguous and specific, and ... it's ultimately rooted in eyewitness accounts."

Gary Habermas, PhD

9. The apostle Paul writes in 1 Corinthians 15:14: "And if Christ has not been raised, our preaching is useless and so is your faith." Why does Paul call the resurrection of Jesus the very linchpin of the Christian faith?

THINK ABOUT THIS!

The Appearances

When they had carried out all that was written about him, they took him down from the cross and laid him in a tomb. But God raised him from the dead, and for many days he was seen by those who had traveled with him from Galilee to Jerusalem. They are now his witnesses to our people.

Acts 13:29 – 31

"Without having a reliable testimony for the emptiness of Jesus' tomb, the early Christian community could not have survived in Jerusalem proclaiming the resurrection of Christ."

German scholar Wolfhart Pannenberg

Early in the morning, Jesus stood on the shore, but the disciples did not realize that it was Jesus. He called out to them, "Friends, haven't you any fish?" "No," they answered. He said, "Throw your net on the right side of the boat and you will find some." When they did, they were unable to haul the net in because of the large number of fish. Then the disciple whom Jesus loved said to Peter, "It is the Lord!" As soon as Simon Peter heard him say, "It is the Lord," he wrapped his outer garment around him (for he had taken it off) and jumped into the water. The other disciples followed in the boat, towing the net full of fish, for they were not far from shore, about a hundred yards. When they landed, they saw a fire of burning coals there with fish on it, and some bread. Jesus said to them, "Bring some of the fish you have just caught." So Simon Peter climbed back into the boat and dragged the net ashore. It was full of large fish, 153, but even with so many the net was not torn. Jesus said to them, "Come and have breakfast." None of the disciples dared ask him, "Who are you?" They knew it was the Lord. Jesus came, took the bread and gave it to them, and did the same with the fish. This was now the third time Jesus appeared to his disciples after he was raised from the dead.

John 21:4 – 14

"The appearances of Jesus are as well authenticated as anything in antiquity ... There can be no rational doubt that they occurred, and that the main reason why Christians became sure of the resurrection in the earliest days was just this. They could say with assurance, 'We have seen the Lord.' They knew it was he."

British theologian Michael Green

"Even the more skeptical historians agree that for primitive Christianity ... the resurrection of Jesus from the dead was a real event in history, the very foundation of faith, and not a mythical idea arising out of the creative imagination of believers."

Historian Carl Braaten

OPTIONAL DISCUSSION QUESTIONS
for Those Investigating Christianity

• Given the severity of the penalty for an escaped prisoner during the Roman era, how motivated were the guards to prevent such an occurrence? How does this fact affect the credibility of the biblical account surrounding Jesus' death and resurrection?

• Even Jesus' enemies acknowledged that the tomb was empty. What weight does this give to the credibility of this claim? Why?

• Everyone in the ancient world admitted the tomb was empty; the issue was how it got that way. Can you think of any logical explanation for the vacant tomb other than the resurrection of Jesus?

• Do you agree or disagree with the following statements? Give reasons for your responses.

  – Jesus' tomb was not really empty.

  – The disciples stole the body.

  – The women went to the wrong tomb.

  – The disciples embellished the story of the empty tomb because they were Jesus' friends.

  – The empty tomb was simply a legend that developed over time.

• Gary Habermas reduced the issue of the resurrection to two questions: Did Jesus die? And was he later seen alive? Based on the evidence so far, how would you answer those questions?

• Could there be any plausible alternatives that could explain away the encounters people had with the risen Jesus? Could these accounts be legendary in nature? Or how likely is it that the witnesses had all experienced the same hallucination?

Between Sessions

Personal Reflection

On his arrival, Jesus found that Lazarus had already been in the tomb for four days. Now Bethany was less than two miles from Jerusalem, and many Jews had come to Martha and Mary to comfort them in the loss of their brother. When Martha heard that Jesus was coming, she went out to meet him, but Mary stayed at home.

"Lord," Martha said to Jesus, "if you had been here, my brother would not have died. But I know that even now God will give you whatever you ask." Jesus said to her, "Your brother will rise again." Martha answered, "I know he will rise again in the resurrection at the last day."

Jesus said to her, "I am the resurrection and the life. The one who believes in me will live, even though they die; and whoever lives by believing in me will never die. Do you believe this?" "Yes, Lord," she replied, "I believe that you are the Messiah, the Son of God, who was to come into the world."...

When Mary reached the place where Jesus was and saw him, she fell at his feet and said, "Lord, if you had been here, my brother would not have died." When Jesus saw her weeping, and the Jews who had come along with her also weeping, he was deeply moved in spirit and troubled. "Where have you laid him?" he asked. "Come and see, Lord," they replied. Jesus wept...

Then Jesus looked up and said, "Father, I thank you that you have heard me. I knew that you always hear me, but I said this for the benefit of the people standing here, that they may believe that you sent me." When he had said this, Jesus called in a loud voice, "Lazarus, come out!" The dead man came out, his hands and feet wrapped with strips of linen, and a cloth around his face. Jesus said to them, "Take off the grave clothes and let him go."

John 11:17–27, 32–35, 41b–44

1. Have you ever lost someone you loved? If so, perhaps you can relate to Martha's feelings of frustration and pain upon seeing Jesus. Were you angry like she was that God didn't intervene in some way to prevent it? Like Martha, do you have a distant hope that your loved one will one day rise again? If so, what leads you to believe that there is life after death? From where does your hope come? Is it simply wishful thinking, or is your hope grounded in reality?

2. Now that you've had a chance to evaluate the evidence, what have you concluded about Jesus' power and authority over death? Did Jesus really return alive from the dead? Was the resurrection a legend, a hoax, or was it an actual event that changed the history of the world? What's your own conclusion concerning whether Jesus' tomb was empty on that first Easter morning, and what does it mean for you personally?

3. *The resurrection is the supreme vindication of Jesus' divine identity and his inspired teaching. It's the proof of his triumph over sin and death. It's the foreshadowing of the eternal resurrection of his followers and the basis of all Christian hope! It's the miracle of all miracles.* Do these statements make sense to you or are they difficult for you to believe? What do you think is significant about the resurrection?

4. Reread the exchange between Jesus and Martha at the beginning of the "Personal Reflection." Claiming he was able to defeat spiritual death and impart eternal life to anyone who believes in him, Jesus asked Martha, "Do you believe this?" The Bible teaches that faith is being sure of what is hoped for and certain of what cannot be seen. Imagine you are in Martha's place and Jesus is asking you the same question. "Do you believe this?" What is *your* response?

5. Whether you believe, disbelieve, or are wrestling with doubts, Jesus is alive today and is willing to meet you wherever you are. Speak to him at this moment and ask him to reveal himself to you.

Personal Reading

Please read the following book content in preparation for session six:

The Case for Christ, conclusion: The Verdict of History

Reaching Your Verdict

Having already considered the persuasive evidence for the empty tomb, and eyewitness accounts of the risen Jesus, it was time for me to seek out any circumstantial evidence that might bolster the case for the resurrection. I knew that if an event as extraordinary as the resurrection of Jesus had really occurred, history would be littered with indirect evidence backing it up.

Lee Strobel

Watch This!

Video Teaching Segment

Space is provided to take notes on anything that stands out to you.

Discuss This!

1. What is the difference between direct evidence and circumstantial (indirect) evidence? Give examples of each. In what ways might circumstantial evidence, such as eyewitness accounts, be just as compelling as direct evidence?

FAST FACT

Circumstantial Evidence

"Eyewitness testimony is called direct evidence because people describe under oath how they personally saw the defendant commit the crime. While this is often compelling, it can sometimes be subject to faded memories, prejudices, and even outright fabrication. In contrast, circumstantial evidence is made up of indirect facts from which inferences can be rationally drawn. Its cumulative effect can be every bit as strong — and in many instances even more potent — than eyewitness accounts ... Circumstantial evidence is plural rather than singular. In other words, it's built brick by brick by brick until there's a sturdy foundation on which conclusions can be confidently based."

Lee Strobel

2. Do you agree that if an event as extraordinary as the resurrection of Jesus had actually occurred, history would be littered with indirect evidence backing it up? Why or why not? Can you give an example of the kind of circumstantial evidence you think would bolster the case for the resurrection? If the resurrection were a hoax, what sort of circumstantial evidence would substantiate that?

The Disciples Were Willing to Suffer and Die for Their Beliefs

"When Jesus was crucified his followers were discouraged and depressed. They no longer had confidence that Jesus had been sent by God, because they believed anyone crucified was accursed by God. They also had been taught that God would not let his Messiah suffer death. So they dispersed. The Jesus movement was all but stopped in its tracks. Then, after a short period of time, we see them abandoning their occupations, regathering, and committing themselves to spreading a very specific message — that Jesus Christ was the Messiah of God who died on a cross, returned to life, and was seen alive by them. And they were willing to spend the rest of their lives proclaiming this, without any payoff from a human point of view. It's not as though there were a mansion awaiting them on the Mediterranean. They faced a life of hardship. They often went without food, slept exposed to the elements, were ridiculed, beaten, imprisoned. And finally, most of them were executed in torturous ways ...

"However, the apostles were willing to die for something they had seen with their own eyes and touched with their own hands. They were in a unique position not to just believe Jesus rose from the dead but to know for sure. And when you've got eleven credible people with no ulterior motives, with nothing to gain and a lot to lose, who all agree they observed something with their own eyes — now you've got some difficulty explaining that away."

J. P. Moreland, PhD

Five times I [Paul] received from the Jews the forty lashes minus one. Three times I was beaten with rods, once I was pelted with stones, three times I was shipwrecked, I spent a night and a day in the open sea, I have been constantly on the move. I have been in danger from rivers, in danger from bandits, in danger from my fellow Jews, in danger from Gentiles; in danger in the city, in danger in the country, in danger at sea; and in danger from false believers. I have labored and toiled and have often gone without sleep; I have known hunger and thirst and have often gone without food; I have been cold and naked.

2 Corinthians 11:24 – 27

3. When Jesus was executed, his disciples became fearful for their lives and they scattered. Their hopes had been dashed because the one they had believed to be the Messiah was murdered by crucifixion under the authority of the Roman Empire. Yet shortly thereafter, the disciples took a stand in Jerusalem proclaiming that Jesus was the Messiah, the very Son of God. If the disciples hadn't really seen Jesus alive, what could account for their change of heart and heroic efforts to spread the gospel? How likely do you think that the disciples were sincere, but sincerely wrong?

"I say unequivocally that the evidence for the resurrection of Jesus Christ is so overwhelming that it compels acceptance by proof which leaves absolutely no room for doubt."
— Sir Lionel Luckhoo, called the world's most successful lawyer by *The Guinness Book of World Records*

THINK ABOUT THIS!

"It had been put to me this way: People will die for their religious beliefs if they sincerely believe they're true, but people won't die for their religious beliefs if they know their beliefs are false. While most people can only have faith that their beliefs are true, the disciples were in a position to know without a doubt whether or not Jesus had risen from the dead. They claimed that they saw him, talked with him, and ate with him. If they weren't absolutely certain, they wouldn't have allowed themselves to be tortured to death for proclaiming that the resurrection had happened."

Lee Strobel

4. Can you think of anyone in history who has knowingly and willingly died for a lie? What degree of certainty would you need before you would be willing to lay down your life for a belief? How thoroughly would you investigate a matter if you were going to base your life on it?

More Circumstantial Evidence

The Conversion of Skeptics

"Another piece of circumstantial evidence is that there were hardened skeptics who didn't believe in Jesus before his crucifixion — and were to some degree dead-set against Christianity — who turned around and adopted the Christian faith after Jesus' death. There's no good reason for this apart from them having experienced the resurrected Christ."

J. P. Moreland, PhD

The Emergence of the Church

"The resurrection was undoubtedly the central proclamation of the early church from the very beginning. The earliest Christians didn't just endorse Jesus' teachings; they were convinced they had seen him alive after his crucifixion. That's what changed their lives and started the church. Certainly, since this was their centermost conviction, they would have made absolutely sure that it was true."

Gary Habermas, PhD

Ongoing Encounters with Christ

"There's one other category of evidence ... It's the ongoing encounter with the resurrected Christ that happens all over the world, in every culture, people from all kinds of backgrounds and personalities — well educated and not, rich and poor, thinkers and feelers, men and women. They all will testify that more than any single thing in their lives, Jesus Christ has changed them. To me, this provides the final evidence — not the only evidence but the final confirming proof — that the message of Jesus can open the door to a direct encounter with the risen Christ."

J. P. Moreland

Lee's Story, Part 1

"I'll admit it: I was ambushed by the amount and quality of the evidence that Jesus is the unique Son of God. As I sat at my desk that Sunday afternoon, I shook my head in amazement. I had seen defendants carted off to the death chamber on much less convincing proof! The cumulative facts and data pointed unmistakably toward a conclusion that I wasn't entirely comfortable in reaching. Frankly, I had wanted to believe that the deification of Jesus was the result of legendary development in which well-meaning but misguided people slowly turned a wise sage into the mythological Son of God. That seemed safe and reassuring; after all, a roving apocalyptic preacher from the first century could make no demands on me. But while I went into my investigation thinking that this legendary explanation was intuitively obvious, I emerged convinced it was totally without basis.

"On November 8, 1981, I realized that my biggest objection to Jesus also had been quieted by the evidence of history. I found myself chuckling at how the tables had been turned. In light of the convincing facts I had learned during my investigation, in the face of this overwhelming avalanche of evidence in the case for Christ, the great irony was this: it would require much more faith for me to maintain my atheism than to trust in Jesus of Nazareth!"

5. Lee's investigation of Christ led him to conclude there is an avalanche of evidence pointing toward the truth of Christianity. Name some of the most convincing pieces of evidence you have discovered.

THINK ABOUT THIS!

Lee's Story, Part 2

"By November 8, 1981, my legend thesis, to which I had doggedly clung for so many years, had been thoroughly dismantled. What's more, my journalistic skepticism toward the supernatural had melted in light of the breathtaking historical evidence that the resurrection of Jesus was a real, historical event. In fact, my mind could not conjure up a single explanation that fit the evidence of history nearly as well as the conclusion that Jesus was who he claimed to be: the one and only Son of God. The atheism I had embraced for so long buckled under the weight of historical truth. It was a stunning and radical outcome, certainly not what I had anticipated when I embarked on this investigative process. But it was, in my opinion, a decision compelled by the facts. All of which led me to the 'So what?' question. If this is true, what difference does it make? There were several obvious implications."

6. Lee identifies the following list of implications to the "So what?" question concerning the true identity of Jesus. How do these statements strike you? What questions do they raise for you? Which of these statements, if true, would make the greatest impact on your life and why?

- If Jesus is the Son of God, his teachings are more than just good ideas from a wise teacher; they are divine insights on which I can confidently build my life.

- If Jesus sets the standard for morality, I can now have an unwavering foundation for my choices and decisions, rather than basing them on the ever-shifting sands of expediency and self-centeredness.

- If Jesus did rise from the dead, he's still alive today and available for me to encounter on a personal basis.

- If Jesus conquered death, he can open the door of eternal life for me too.

- If Jesus has divine power, he has the supernatural ability to guide me and help me and transform me as I follow him.

- If Jesus personally knows the pain of loss and suffering, he can comfort and encourage me in the midst of the turbulence that he himself warned is inevitable in a world corrupted by sin.

cont.

- If Jesus loves me as he says, he has my best interests at heart. That means I have nothing to lose and everything to gain by committing myself to him and his purposes.
- If Jesus is who he claims to be (and remember, no leader of any other major religion has even pretended to be God), as my Creator he rightfully deserves my allegiance, obedience, and worship.

THINK ABOUT THIS!

Lee's Story, Part 3

"After a personal investigation that spanned more than six hundred days and count-less hours, my own verdict in the case for Christ was clear. However, as I sat at my desk, I realized that I needed more than an intellectual decision. I wanted to take the experiential step that J. P. Moreland had described in my interview with him. Looking for a way to bring that about, I reached over to a Bible and opened it to John 1:12, a verse I had encountered during my investigation: 'Yet to all who did receive him, to those who believed in his name, he gave the right to become children of God.' The key verbs in that verse spell out with mathematical precision what it takes to go beyond mere mental assent to Jesus' deity and enter into an ongoing relationship with him by becoming adopted into God's family: believe + receive = become."

7. According to John 1:12 (see the "Think About This!" box above), what does it take to become a child of God? What does it mean to *believe* in Jesus Christ? What do you think it means to *receive* Jesus into your life? What does it mean to *become* a child of God?

Lee's Story, Part 4

"When I read in the Bible that my sins separated me from God, who is holy and morally pure, this resonated as being true. Certainly God, whose existence I had denied for years, seemed extremely distant, and it became obvious to me that I needed the cross of Jesus to bridge that gulf. Said the apostle Peter, 'For Christ also suffered once for sins, the righteous for the unrighteous, to bring you to God' (1 Peter 3:18).

"Every other faith system I studied during my investigation was based on the 'do' plan. In other words, it was necessary for people to do something — for example, use a Tibetan prayer wheel, pay alms, go on pilgrimages, undergo reincarnations, work off karma from past misdeeds, reform their character — to try to somehow earn their way back to God. Despite their best efforts, lots of sincere people just wouldn't make it. Christianity is unique. It's based on the 'done' plan — Jesus has done for us on the cross what we cannot do for ourselves: he has paid the death penalty that we deserve for our rebellion and wrongdoing, so we can become reconciled with God."

8. To what extent can you relate to Lee's sense of being separated from God because of sin? Lee explains that every other faith system is based on the "do" plan, but Christianity alone is based on what has already been "done." Read his comments in the "Think About This!" box above and summarize his points in your own words. What is it that Jesus did on the cross that we cannot do for ourselves?

THINK ABOUT THIS!

Lee's Story, Part 5

"Once the 'believe' part of John 1:12 is firmly in place; all that's left is to 'receive' Jesus' grace, and then you'll become his son or daughter, engaged in a spiritual adventure that can flourish for the rest of your life and into eternity.

"So on November 8, 1981, I talked with God in a heartfelt and unedited prayer, admitting and turning from my wrongdoing, and receiving the gift of forgiveness and eternal life through Jesus. I told him that with his help I wanted to follow him and his ways from here on out. There were no lightning bolts, no audible replies, no tingly sensations. I know that some people feel a rush of emotion at such a moment; as for me, however, there was something else that was equally exhilarating: there was the rush of reason.

"Looking back nearly two decades, I can see with clarity that the day I personally made a decision in the case for Christ was nothing less than the pivotal event of my entire life. After taking that step, I knew from John 1:12 that I had crossed the threshold into a new experience. I had 'become' something different: a child of God, forever adopted into his family through the historical, risen Jesus. Said the apostle Paul, 'Therefore, if anyone is in Christ, the new creation has come: The old has gone, the new is here' (2 Corinthians 5:17)."

10. What is your verdict in the case for Christ? To what extent has the evidence presented in these sessions (and the book) been sufficient for you to draw a final conclusion? If you haven't already, are you willing to take a step in the direction the evidence is pointing and place your faith and trust in Jesus Christ, receiving him into your life? If not, what obstacles or barriers are most holding you back? What kinds of questions remain for you?

For it is by grace you have been saved, through faith — and this not from yourselves, it is the gift of God — not by works, so that no one can boast.
(Ephesians 2:8 – 9)

OPTIONAL DISCUSSION QUESTIONS
for Those Investigating Christianity

• J. P. Moreland suggests that it is very difficult to explain away the radical transformation of people who were originally skeptical about Jesus and then believed in him after the resurrection. Do you agree with this reasoning? Why or why not? What might have led to the radical transformation of such skeptics as James, the brother of Jesus, and Paul, formerly known as Saul?

• If Jesus had *not* risen from the grave, what did the disciples have to gain—money, power, or status—by falsely professing that he had?

• Besides the resurrection, what might account for the rapid spread of Christianity in spite of the shameful death of its founder and the dispersion of the disciples?

• What is the difference between the early disciples who were tortured and/or killed for refusing to renounce their beliefs and suicide bombers today who take their own lives in an attempt to kill others based on their beliefs?

• How do the claims of people worldwide who say they've had a personal experience with the risen Christ influence your opinion of the circumstantial evidence of the case for Christ? Have you ever personally observed someone transform in behavior and character after coming to believe in Jesus Christ? What is your view of people who make such claims?

In the Coming Days

Personal Reflection

Yet to all who did receive him, to those who believed in his name, he gave the right to become children of God.

John 1:12

BELIEVE + RECEIVE = BECOME

1. To what extent have you been able to set aside your biases and preconceived notions and approach the evidence in these discussions as a fair and impartial juror in the case for Christ? In the end, the verdict is yours and yours alone. Nobody else can cast the ballot for you.

2. After examining the experts, considering the arguments, and discussing your concerns, maybe you have the "believe" part of the above equation down, and all that's left for you is to "receive" the forgiveness, grace, and leadership of Jesus Christ in your life. What does it mean for you to receive Jesus? How might this impact your life? How does the idea of becoming a son or daughter of God make you feel? Does it seem a little mystical or does it fill you with hope and wonder? Are you willing to take that step in a simple, unrehearsed prayer to God right now?

3. Or, on the other hand, do you still have lingering questions, doubts, or concerns? Perhaps the case isn't conclusive and you have unresolved issues that haven't been addressed. If so, are you willing to continue on in your investigative journey by checking out some of the related resources suggested in the book? Or if you've benefited from this format, your next step might be to consider a discussion on *The Case for Faith* or *The Case for a Creator.*

4. Whatever your conclusion, are you willing to make this a front-burner issue in your life? If Jesus really is who he claimed to be, your eternal life hinges on it, for as he himself said, "If you do not believe that I am he, you will indeed die in your sins" (John 8:24). These are sobering words, but they were offered by Jesus out of an authentic and loving concern for each one of us. So we urge you to consider carefully and seriously all of the evidence presented and ultimately answer this final question: *Have you reached your verdict in the case for Christ?*

Jesus [said], "I am the way and the truth and the life. No one comes to the Father except through me."

John 14:6

For God so loved the world that he gave his one and only Son, that whoever believes in him shall not perish but have eternal life.

John 3:16

Small Group Leader Helps

To ensure a successful small group experience, read the following information before beginning.

Group Preparation

Whether your small group has been meeting together for years or is gathering for the first time, be sure to designate a consistent time and place to work through the six sessions. Once you establish the when and where of your times together, select a facilitator who will keep discussions on track and an eye on the clock. If you choose to rotate this responsibility, assign the six sessions to their respective facilitators up front, so that group members can prepare their thoughts and questions prior to the session they are responsible for leading. Follow the same assignment procedure should your group want to serve any snacks or beverages.

A Note to Facilitators

As facilitator, you are responsible for honoring the agreed-upon time frame of each meeting, for prompting helpful discussion among your group, and for keeping the dialogue equitable by drawing out quieter members and helping more talkative members to remember that others' insights are valued in your group.

You might find it helpful to preview each session's video teaching segment and then scan the discussion questions that pertain to it, highlighting various questions that you want to be sure to cover during your group's meeting. Ask God in advance of your time together to guide your group's discussion, and then be sensitive to the direction he wishes to lead.

Urge participants to bring their study guide, pen, and a Bible to every gathering. Encourage them to consider buying a copy of *The Case for Christ* book by Lee Strobel to supplement this study.

Session Format

Each session of the study guide includes the following group components:

- **Watch This!** — Space is provided for individual notes and insights as the group views the session's video presentation, about 30 minutes.

- **Discuss This!** — Video-related and Bible exploration questions reinforce the session content and elicit personal input from every group member. The boxed content ("Think About This!" and "Fast Fact") interspersed throughout this section bears directly on surrounding questions. Either have group members read this content to themselves, read it aloud yourself, or have group members take turns reading it aloud. The latter two options will take longer.

- **Optional Discussion Questions for Those Investigating Christianity** — At the end of the main discussion section are further questions for groups that have more time or interest. You may even choose to substitute a question or two for questions in the main discussion section.

Additionally, in each session you will find a **Between Sessions** section (**In the Coming Days** after session six) that includes suggestions for personal reflection and response as well as recommended reading from *The Case for Christ* book in preparation for the next session.

The Case for Christ

A Journalist's Personal Investigation of the Evidence for Jesus

Lee Strobel
New York Times *Bestselling Author*

A Seasoned Journalist Chases Down the Biggest Story in History

Is there credible evidence that Jesus of Nazareth really is the Son of God?

Retracing his own spiritual journey from atheism to faith, Lee Strobel, former legal editor of the *Chicago Tribune*, cross-examines a dozen experts with doctorates from schools like: Cambridge, Princeton, and Brandeis who are recognized authorities in their own fields.

Strobel challenges them with questions like: How reliable is the New Testament? Does evidence for Jesus exist outside the Bible? Is there any reason to believe the resurrection was an actual event?

Strobel's tough, point-blank questions make this Gold Medallion-winning book read like a captivating, fast-paced novel. But it's not fiction. It's a riveting quest for the truth about history's most compelling figure.

What will your verdict be in *The Case for Christ*?

"Lee Strobel probes with bulldog-like tenacity the evidence for the truth of biblical Christianity."

Bruce M. Metzger, PhD, Professor of New Testament,
Emeritus, Princeton Theological Seminary

"Lee Strobel asks the questions a tough-minded skeptic would ask. His book is so good I read it out loud to my wife evenings after dinner. Every inquirer should have it."

Phillip E. Johnson, Law Professor, University of California at Berkeley

Available in stores and online!

ZONDERVAN®
.com

The Case for Christ for Kids Curriculum

Investigating the Truth about Jesus

Lee Strobel with
Christopher D. Hudson

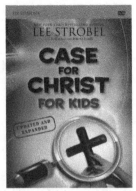

How would the kids in your children's ministry answer friends who ask questions like: Was Jesus really born in a stable? Did his friends tell the truth? Did he really come back from the dead?

In these six lessons children will learn answers to these and other pressing questions in kid-friendly language that will help them grow in their faith. Packed full of well-researched, reliable, and fun investigations of some of the biggest questions kids have, *The Case for Christ for Kids Curriculum* brings Jesus to life by addressing the existence, miracles, ministry, and resurrection of Christ.

This DVD-ROM makes your children's ministry planning simple and includes everything you need for a successful Sunday school, children's church, or VBS program:

- A checklist to help leaders organize each week's study
- Lesson Plans
- Family Pages
- Promotional materials
- AND a VBS expansion kit to help leaders teach *The Case for Christ for Kids Curriculum* as a Vacation Bible School or Backyard Bible Club program

The six sessions include:

- The Case of the Promised Baby
- The Case of the Voice from Heaven
- The Case of the Eyewitnesses
- The Case of the Wedding Crisis
- The Case of the Living Water
- The Case of the Risen Jesus

Available in stores and online!

ZONDERVAN®
.com

The Case for Faith: A DVD Study

Investigating the Toughest Objections to Christianity

Lee Strobel and Garry Poole

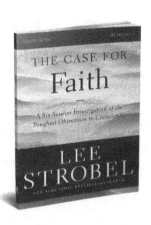

Does believing in Christ mean refusing to ask hard questions in the midst of doubt?

Doubt is familiar territory for Lee Strobel, the former atheist and award-winning author of books for skeptics and Christians. But he believes that faith and reason go hand in hand, and that Christianity is a defensible religion.

In this six-session revised small group video Bible study, Strobel explores the most common emotional obstacles to faith in Christ. These include the natural inclination to wrestle with faith and doubt, the troubling presence of evil and suffering in the world, and the exclusivity of the Christian gospel. They also include this compelling question: *Can I doubt and be a Christian?*

Through compelling personal stories and experts testimony combined with reflection and interaction, Christians and spiritual seekers will learn how to overcome these obstacles, deepen their spiritual convictions, and find new confidence that Christianity is a reasonable faith.

Sessions include:
- The Challenge of Faith
- Dealing with Doubt
- Evil and Suffering, Part 1
- Evil and Suffering, Part 2
- Why Is Jesus the Only Way to God?
- The Power of Faith

Available in stores and online!

ZONDERVAN®
.com

The Case for a Creator: A DVD Study

Investigating the Scientific Evidence That Points toward God

Lee Strobel and Garry Poole

"My road to atheism was paved by science . . . But, ironically, so was my later journey to God." — **Lee Strobel**

Former atheist Lee Strobel has discovered that science, far from being the enemy of faith, now provides a solid foundation for belief in God. New scientific discoveries point to the incredible complexity of our universe, a complexity best explained by the existence of a Creator.

This revised six-session video and separate study guide invites participants to encounter this evidence delivered in a compelling conversational style. Join Strobel in reexamining the theories that once led him away from God. Pastors and small group leaders seeking resources that answer tough questions about the existence of God will find compelling answers in *The Case for a Creator: A DVD Study.*

The six sessions include:
- Science and God
- Doubts about Darwinism
- The Evidence of Cosmology
- The Fine-tuning of the Universe
- The Evidence of Biochemistry
- DNA and the Origin of Life

Available in stores and online!

ZONDERVAN®
.com

Share Your Thoughts

With the Author: Your comments will be forwarded to the author when you send them to *zauthor@zondervan.com*.

With Zondervan: Submit your review of this book by writing to *zreview@zondervan.com*.

Free Online Resources at
www.zondervan.com

Daily Bible Verses and Devotions: Enrich your life with daily Bible verses or devotions that help you start every morning focused on God. Visit www.zondervan.com/newsletters.

Free Email Publications: Sign up for newsletters on Christian living, academic resources, church ministry, fiction, children's resources, and more. Visit www.zondervan.com/newsletters.

Zondervan Bible Search: Find and compare Bible passages in a variety of translations at www.zondervanbiblesearch.com.

Other Benefits: Register to receive online benefits like coupons and special offers, or to participate in research.

ZONDERVAN®